French Army Approaches to Networked Warfare

MICHAEL SHURKIN, RAPHAEL S. COHEN, ARTHUR CHAN

T0308647

Prepared for the United States Army
Approved for public release; distribution unlimited

RAND ARROYO CENTER

For more information on this publication, visit **www.rand.org/t/RR2946**.

About RAND

The RAND Corporation is a research organization that develops solutions to public policy challenges to help make communities throughout the world safer and more secure, healthier and more prosperous. RAND is nonprofit, nonpartisan, and committed to the public interest. To learn more about RAND, visit www.rand.org.

Research Integrity

Our mission to help improve policy and decisionmaking through research and analysis is enabled through our core values of quality and objectivity and our unwavering commitment to the highest level of integrity and ethical behavior. To help ensure our research and analysis are rigorous, objective, and nonpartisan, we subject our research publications to a robust and exacting quality-assurance process; avoid both the appearance and reality of financial and other conflicts of interest through staff training, project screening, and a policy of mandatory disclosure; and pursue transparency in our research engagements through our commitment to the open publication of our research findings and recommendations, disclosure of the source of funding of published research, and policies to ensure intellectual independence. For more information, visit www.rand.org/about/research-integrity.

RAND's publications do not necessarily reflect the opinions of its research clients and sponsors.

Cover: Photo by Sgt. Thomas Childs.

Background illustration: BAIVECTOR/Adobe Stock.

Preface

This report documents research and analysis conducted as part of a project entitled *Learning from the French Army's Experience with Networked Warfare*, sponsored by the Office of the Deputy Chief of Staff, G-8, U.S. Army. The purpose of the project was to examine the French Army's approach to networked warfare and learn from its experience developing and fielding key components of its networked warfare system, including the extent to which the French have found that the technology delivers on its promised benefits, and whether or how it has changed the way the French fight.

This research was conducted within RAND Arroyo Center's Strategy, Doctrine, and Resources Program. RAND Arroyo Center, part of the RAND Corporation, is a federally funded research and development center (FFRDC) sponsored by the United States Army.

RAND operates under a "Federal-Wide Assurance" (FWA00003425) and complies with the *Code of Federal Regulations for the Protection of Human Subjects Under United States Law* (45 CFR 46), also known as "the Common Rule," as well as with the implementation guidance set forth in U.S. Department of Defense (DoD) Instruction 3216.02. As applicable, this compliance includes reviews and approvals by RAND's Institutional Review Board (the Human Subjects Protection Committee) and by the U.S. Army. The views of sources utilized in this study are solely their own and do not represent the official policy or position of DoD or the U.S. Government.

Contents

Figures and Tables

Figures

Tables

Summary

The research reported here was completed in February 2019, followed by security review by the U.S. Army sponsor and the Office of the Chief of Public Affairs, with final sign-off in May 2022.

The French Army has been developing and fielding networked warfare technology since the 1990s and now boasts both considerable experience using the technology in the field (including in combat in Afghanistan and the Sahel) and a successful modernization program. As part of an effort to glean lessons learned from the French program and experience with network-centric warfare (NCW) for the U.S. Army, we combed through primary and secondary French sources and interviewed several dozen French Army officers, think tank analysts, and government experts.

The concept of NCW dates to the early 1990s and is closely tied to a set of ideas about the effects of the evolution of technology and precision weapons on warfare concepts. NCW's central thesis argued that, because of information networks, the power and lethality of a deployed force could be greater than the sum of its parts; information, moreover, would enable modern forces to forgo armor and mass. Theorists in the United States believed that the technology was precipitating a so-called Revolution in Military Affairs.

France decided to follow the United States' lead in developing networked warfare technology, but less out of enthusiasm for its benefits than a sense that it had to keep up with the U.S. military to remain relevant. French military leaders believed that networked warfare technology would improve their army's capabilities, but they had already redesigned their military and were interested in the technology only to the extent that it complemented existing efforts. Moreover, they estimated that an incremental approach would be more affordable as well as sufficient, and therefore declined to bet heavily on the technology at the outset.

The French military developed several systems and fielded them in real time, which helped it accrue experience. In 2014, drawing on lessons from its experience and attempting to meet the need for a large-scale armored vehicle modernization program, France embarked on an effort—the SCORPION program—to replace the technology it already had developed with a second generation while developing and fielding new armored vehicles. The technology developed up to that point often is referred to as *la numérisation de l'espace de bataille* (NEB) 1.0, or "digitization of the battle space." SCORPION-era technology sometimes is referred to as "NEB 2.0."

French NEB 1.0 technology consists of various information systems, from communications gear worn by individual soldiers and networking systems mounted on armored vehicles to systems used by brigade levels and above. France has fielded at least some of this technology in every deployment since 2006—for example, in Afghanistan, the Central African Republic, Côte d'Ivoire, Lebanon, and the Sahel, as well as in routine training exercises. In the process, France has been able to assess some of its strengths and weaknesses. In general, French military leaders find that NEB 1.0 technology has improved their capabilities, although not in a dramatic way. Such leaders also note that many of their systems were developed independently for specific purposes, often by different contractors. The bridges linking such systems are adequate at best. The lack of integration—or conviviality, as the French term it—among the systems, their poor ergonomics (specifically, the lack of user-friendly interfaces), and a cultural reluctance to use the technology have resulted in mixed reviews of the systems by French officers, who tend to speak of them in positive but qualified language. SCORPION is intended to improve on the extant technology by replacing multiple systems with a single system and by building interoperability into the various components from the beginning. SCORPION systems, which include a new broadband radio, will enable *embarked simulation*, meaning that vehicle crews could run through simulations while networked with other vehicles, as well as engage in collaborative warfare. *Collaborative warfare* refers to the ability of vehicles to automatically share such information as the location of a detected threat with vehicles on the network that might be in a better position to neutralize the threat than the vehicle that detected it, ideally with vehicles with *slew to cue* capabilities—the ability to have a vehicle's gun or other weapon system move automatically to target a threat upon reception of targeting data. French officers are optimistic that the new gear will go far toward delivering on the long-expected benefits of NCW technology.

French officers found that some of the expected benefits of the technology in NEB 1.0 were valid, although they estimated the overall value to be less than hoped. Advantages of the technology are its abilities to speed up the decision cycle and make forces more reactive. French officers have high regard for the benefits of Blue Force tracking and are impressed by the potential benefits for logistics and sustainment. By no means, however, do they believe that the technology changes how they operate in any fundamental way.

The French experience with NCW also identifies several key deficiencies. French military leaders found that NEB 1.0 technology is too difficult to use and is poorly integrated among different systems. However, they are optimistic that SCORPION will address those problems. French officers also are uncertain about the value of the technology in any environment in which it is degraded, as it likely would be when fighting an adversary with robust electronic warfare capabilities or an adversary that is savvy enough to know how to deceive or game the technology. Even in the best-case scenario, French officials argued that the NEB 1.0 technology does little to lift the fog of war with respect to the adversary. Finally, the French Army has not tested its technology at a scale larger than a brigade. The French Army also found that this technology creates problems with respect to interoperability with partners and allies.

Many of the French Army's concerns about NCW, however, are about the cultural second-order effects of technology. On one hand, French Army officers believe that there is an institutional reluctance to embrace technology, something that will need to change over time. On the other hand, French officers worry about the risk of overdependence on the technology and that French commanders might mistake the partial information they see for precise and complete information. Some also worry that the technology will lead to greater centralization and micromanagement, which are contrary to the French Army's current emphasis on autonomous action by lower-echelon commanders (or *subsidiarité*). Others, however, argue that the strong institutional culture that resists micromanagement will shield the French Army from this effect.

What the U.S. Army Can Learn from the French Experience

Ultimately, the French experience offers insufficient grounds for the U.S. Army to reconsider its approach to NCW. If anything, the French experience likely reaffirms—although it may not decisively prove (given that the French Army has yet to fully test NEB 2.0 in high-end combat)—the U.S. Army's skepticism about the central tenet of the 1990s version of the Revolution in Military Affairs, which was that better information-sharing would compensate for mass, firepower, and protection.

This report does not yield unambiguous conclusions about what systems the U.S. Army should procure. During the course of this research effort, we did not conduct more-detailed field testing and engineering analyses of French and comparable American systems needed to make such recommendations and, at a basic level, the U.S. Army and French Army are trying to solve different problems. Interviews with French Army officers suggest that the equipment is mostly a French solution to a French problem stemming from French budgetary constraints—specifically, the need to build one middle-weight force that is deployable to Africa (given France's weak logistical capabilities compared with those of the United States) but is still robust enough for higher-end threats. By contrast, the U.S. Army's modernization challenge starts with a different strategic premise—deterring China and Russia—and makes different assumptions about available logistical capabilities.[1] The two militaries' requirements, therefore, do not necessarily overlap sufficiently for a solution appropriate for one to be appropriate for the other.

---

[1]   U.S. Department of Defense, *Summary of the 2018 National Defense Strategy of the United States of America: Sharpening the American Military's Competitive Edge*, Washington, D.C., January 2018, p. 1.

Nonetheless, the French experience with NCW and the French Army's modernization effort yield a handful of lessons for the U.S. Army. First, especially in comparison with the U.S. Army's modernization program of the 1990s, the French Army moderated its ambitions, settling for building a force that was better than what it had rather than aiming for wholesale transformation. Ultimately, this approach proved more practical and, arguably, more successful. Second, the French experience underscores the need to explicitly weigh trade-offs between the risk of failure in an ambitious wholesale approach to modernization and the risk of incompatibility inherent in an incremental approach to procuring new technologies, especially communication technologies. Third, French modernization benefited from fielding and testing new technologies early in the process, which allowed the French Army to inject lessons learned back into the development process. Fourth, the French modernization program highlights the importance of incorporating the human dimension—focusing on not only how to make technology user-friendly but also how technology will affect organizational culture—into the design process. Finally, despite the focus on modernization and technology, the French experience underscores the importance of training armies to fight without the technology. For the French Army, the latter point is a matter of organizational, cultural, and institutional pride, but for the U.S. Army, which is focused on a fight with a near-peer competitor with the ability to disrupt the network, the ability to fight without these technologies may be an operational imperative.

Acknowledgments

This report would not have been possible without the assistance of many people. First, we thank Timothy Muchmore of the Quadrennial Defense Review Office, U.S. Army for sponsoring and guiding the research. Former RAND Arroyo Center Strategy, Doctrine, and Resources program director, Sally Sleeper, and associate program directors, Steve Watts and Jennifer Kavanagh, provided valuable leadership throughout the research process. Our RAND colleagues Dan Gonzales, Christopher Pernin, and Abby Doll helped shape our thinking about this subject and provided valuable technical input for this report. Tom McNaugher of Georgetown University and Danielle Tarraf of RAND provided thoughtful feedback on an earlier draft of this report and improved it considerably. French Army Colonel (retired) Bertrand Darras was an invaluable member of the research team, helping us think through our research design, organizing our research trip to France, and commenting on a draft of this report. The United States Defense Attaché Office at U.S. Embassy Paris assisted us with gaining access to the French military. We also owe a special debt of gratitude to General Bernard Barrera for approving our project and granting us access to serving military officers, and to General Charles Beaudouin for his continued support and for his willingness to be accessible to us. Finally, we are grateful to the dozens of French military officers, think tank analysts, and journalists who volunteered their time to be interviewed for this report. Although human subjects protection protocols prohibit us from listing them by name, their frank and open insights form the cornerstone of our empirical research, and we cannot thank them enough.

Abbreviations

AAN	Army After Next
ATLAS	*l'automatisation des tirs et liaisons de l'artillerie sol/sol*
BFT	Blue Force Tracker
CJEF	Combined Joint Expeditionary Force
DGA	*Direction général de l'armament,* or Directorate-General of Armaments
DoD	U.S. Department of Defense
EBRC	*Engin blindé de reconnaissance et de combat,* or armored reconnaissance and combat vehicle, also known as Jaguar
FCS	Future Combat Systems
FELIN	*Fantassin à équipements et liaisons intégrés,* or Integrated Infantryman Equipment and Communications
GAMSTAT	*Groupement aéro mobilité de la section technique de l'armée de Terre,* or Air Mobility Grouping of the Technical Section of the Army
GTIA	*Groupement Tactique Interarmes,* or Combined Arms Tactical Group
HF	high frequency
IFRI	Institut Français des Relations Internationales
MR	Mission Restricted
MS	Mission Secret
MTR	Military Technical Revolution
NCW	network-centric warfare
NEB	*numérisation de l'espace de bataille,* or digitization of the battle space

NUMESIM	*numérisation simplifiée pour les hélicoptères de l'armée de terre*, or simplified digitization for Army helicopters
PR4G	*poste radio de quatrième génération*, or fourth-generation radio set
RETEX	*Retour d'Expérience*
RMA	Revolution in Military Affairs
SCORPION	*Synergie du contact renforcée par la polyvalence et l'infovalorisation*, or contact synergy reinforced by flexibility and "infovalorisation," roughly translatable to "getting the full value out of information"
SGTIA	*Sous-groupement tactique interarmes*, or combined arms tactical subgroup
SIA	*Système d'information des armées*, or joint information system
SICAT	*Système informatique de communication de l'armée de terre*, or Army communication information system
SICF	*Système d'information pour le commandement des forces*, or information system for the French command
SICS	SCORPION Information and Combat System
SIR	*Système d'information régimentaire*, or regimental information system
SIT	*Système d'information terminal*, or terminal information system
SITALAT	*Système d'information terminal de l'aviation légère de l'armée de Terre*
SIT COMDÉ	*Système d'Information Terminal du COMbattant DÉbarqué*
SITEL	*Systèmes d'information terminaux élémentaires*
STAT	*Section Technique de l'Armée de Terre*, or Army technical section
TRADOC	U.S. Army Training and Doctrine Command
VAB	*Véhicle de l'avant blindé*, or forward armored vehicle
VBCI	*Véhicle blindé de combat d'infanterie*, or armored infantry combat vehicle
VBMR	*Véhicle blindé multi-roles*, or multi-role armored vehicle, also known as Griffon
VHF	very high frequency

CHAPTER ONE

Introduction and Methodology

To a U.S. military audience, *networked warfare* and *network-centric warfare* (NCW) are loaded—if somewhat antiquated—terms. They hearken back to the debates over U.S. military modernization of the late 1990s and early 2000s and conjure up then–U.S. Secretary of Defense Donald Rumsfeld's push toward military transformation and its promises of radically different ways of fighting wars with a smaller, leaner force. These terms also bring to mind the failure of the massively expensive Future Combat Systems program. Although some of the principles and technologies behind U.S. NCW exist today, the terms themselves arguably are no longer in vogue in U.S. defense circles. They have been replaced with such new operational terms as *multi-domain operations*. And yet, in other militaries, NCW lives on and is still at the fore-front of modernization debates.

In this report, we examine the French Army's adoption of NCW as part of its overall modernization effort. We describe how France employed a more modest theory of NCW and proceeded to develop, procure, and field NCW technology. We draw lessons from the French experience and highlight the implications for the U.S. Army and the Joint Force more broadly. The remainder of this chapter frames the study. First, we define NCW. Next, we briefly outline the rise and fall of NCW in the U.S. context as a foil to the French effort. Finally, the chapter concludes by outlining the report's methodology and structure.

Network-Centric Warfare Defined

Credit for introducing the term *network-centric warfare* usually goes to VADM Arthur K. Cebrowski, later the president of the Naval War College and director of the U.S. Department of Defense's (DoD's) Office of Force Transformation, and John J. Garstka, who in January 1998 published "Network-Centric Warfare: Its Origin and Future," in *Proceedings*, the U.S. Navy's professional journal. The term, as they used it, refers to "network-centric computing" and the application of information technology concepts to warfighting.[1] According to Ronald O'Rourke, "NCW focuses on using computers, high-speed data links, and networking software to link military personnel, platforms, and formations into highly integrated local and wide-area networks."[2] As in network-centric computing, the whole becomes more than the sums of its parts. Specifically, by seamlessly sharing information across platforms, the network is more powerful than the sum of the individual platforms—tanks, ships, or airplanes—that compose the network. Instead, combat power comes from the ability to share information rapidly across the entire force, so that any one platform can leverage the full capabilities of the others.[3]

More broadly, however, the term refers to a set of ideas that rose to dominance in certain U.S. military circles in the 1990s that focused on the kind of force the Army should have, how it should organize that force, and how it should fight. As we shall see, it is those ideas that in some cases distinguish French thinking from the American approach.

A Brief History of the U.S. View of Network-Centric Warfare

Revolution in Military Affairs

The U.S. military began experimenting with digitalization years earlier, but the story of the U.S. military's embrace of NCW began in earnest with the 1990–1991 Persian Gulf War, from which some officials deduced lessons about the significance of new technologies deployed by U.S. forces. Among these observers were Andrew Krepinevich and Andrew Marshall, then the director of DoD's Office of Net Assessment.[4] According to unpublished RAND research, Marshall concluded that the Gulf War validated the Soviet idea from the 1980s that a major paradigm shift in warfare was taking place, one brought on by the evolution of precision stand-off weapons, wide-area sensors, and computerized command and control. In 1991, Marshall tasked Krepinevich with writing what became known as the Military Technical Revolution (MTR) report, with the

---

[1]   Arthur K. Cebrowski and John J. Garstka, "Network-Centric Warfare: Its Origin and Future," *Proceedings*, Vol. 124, January 1998; Fred Stein, John Garska, and Philip L. McIndoo, "Network-Centric Warfare: Impact on Army Operations," *IEEE/AFCEA EUROCOMM 2000: Information Systems for Enhanced Public Safety and Security Proceedings*, 2000, p. 289.

[2]   Ronald O'Rourke, *Navy Network-Centric Warfare Concept: Key Programs and Issues for Congress*, Washington, D.C.: Congressional Research Service, RS20557, May 31, 2005, p. 1.

[3]   Cebrowski and Garstka, 1998, p. 7.

[4]   See Marshall's forward to Andrew F. Krepinevich, Jr., *The Military-Technical Revolution: A Preliminary Assessment*, Washington, D.C.: Center for Strategic and Budgetary Assessments, 2002, p. i, as well as Krepinevich's own account in the introduction, p. iii. A fuller discussion of the history and development of the Revolution in Military Affairs can be found in Thomas K. Adams, *The Army After Next: The First Postindustrial Army*, Stanford, Calif.: Stanford University Press, 2008, pp. 12–33.

term "MTR" taken from Soviet parlance. Marshall substituted the term "revolution in military affairs" for MTR in a July 1993 memo on the subject.[5] Although they saw that technological innovations were important, Marshall and Krepinevich had in mind a paradigm shift about how technology should be implemented and how militaries should reinvent themselves and their doctrines to make the most of the new technology. In 1994, Krepinevich published a more accessible version of his MTR report in *The National Interest*.[6]

Krepinevich and Marshall argued that the world appeared to be "near the beginning of the real revolution in military affairs" because of information technology.[7] This, they believed, enabled armies to accumulate, communicate, process, and act on information at a significantly greater scale and speed than ever before. Militaries could, with unprecedented skill, "identify, prioritize, and attack effectively the military functions that comprise an enemy's 'center of gravity,'" meaning the targets that, "if destroyed, will fatally compromise a state's ability, or will, to block its adversary from achieving its political objectives."[8] War would become more precise, surgical, and, in a way, economical:

> The effect could be to drive conventional military operations from sequential engagements toward a single, simultaneous engagement focused directly on the enemy's center of gravity. Combined with the right intelligence on the essential elements of any enemy target base, it may be possible to attack directly those functions the enemy values most, rather than focusing primarily on his forces. Thus, future conflicts could witness military forces striking directly at the enemy's "jugular," or "central nervous system," at the outset of a conflict without first having to defeat the bulk of his military forces. Conventional operations could produce relatively prompt "strategic" consequences. But this requires the integration of technologically intensive combat and information systems either globally, or within a theater of operations, to achieve a "critical mass" of military effectiveness.[9]

This can be regarded as an early formulation of what would later be described as "effects-based" operations. Rather than undertake the big task of destroying the enemy force head-on, one might instead identify some vulnerability, that, if struck with a limited but focused force, could achieve the same objective as destroying the force alto-

---

[5] Andrew W. Marshall, "Some Thoughts on Military Revolutions," ONA memorandum for record, July 27, 1993, p. 1.

[6] Andrew F. Krepinevich, "Cavalry to Computer: The Pattern of Military Revolutions," *The National Interest*, October 1994.

[7] Andrew W. Marshall, "Some Thoughts on Military Revolutions—Second Version," ONA memorandum for record, August 23, 1993, p. 3.

[8] Krepinevich, 2002, p. 11.

[9] Krepinevich, 2002, p. 12.

gether. Fighting that way would require smarts and speed, but not mass. The appeal of this vision at a time of shrinking end strength is easy to understand.

In 1994, U.S. Army Training and Doctrine Command (TRADOC) made the Revolution in Military Affairs (RMA) into Army dogma in its Pamphlet 525-5, entitled *Force XXI*.[10] From that point until after the second invasion of Iraq in 2003, the focus of the Army's modernization efforts—nearly everything from procurement programs to changes in force structure—would be on making the RMA a reality. This would mean not only developing and integrating the technology but also—and in a manner consistent with Marshall and Krepinevich's thinking about what constituted an RMA—reinventing how the Army organized itself and fought.

The TRADOC pamphlet all but copies Marshall and Krepinevich's concept of RMA. Perhaps the one new thing is the concept of networked operations, denoted in the pamphlet by the term "internetted." For example, the following passage asserts that everything related to warfare is being upended because of technology:

> Information technology is expected to make a thousandfold advance over the next 20 years. In fact, the pace of development is so great that it renders our current material management and acquisition system inadequate. Developments in information technology will revolutionize—and indeed have begun to revolutionize—how nations, organizations, and people interact. The rapid diffusion of information, enabled by these technological advances, challenges the relevance of traditional organizational and management principles. The military implications of new organizational sciences that examine internetted, nonhierarchical versus hierarchical management models are yet to be fully understood. Clearly, Information Age technology, and the management ideas it fosters, will greatly influence military operations in two areas—one evolutionary, the other revolutionary; one we understand, one with which we are just beginning to experiment.[11]

TRADOC identified two ways in which the new technology would affect military operations. First, "future information technology will greatly increase the volume, accuracy, and speed of battlefield information available to commanders." This would "allow organizations to operate at levels most adversaries cannot match, while simultaneously protecting that capability."[12] Second, the changes, which TRADOC called an RMA, obliged the Army to rethink how it managed battles and conducted command and control. Future military operations would "involve the coexistence of both hierarchical and internetted, nonhierarchical processes." Everything would be decentralized, or, to be more precise, "[c]ombinations of centralized and decentralized means will

---

[10] TRADOC, *Force XXI Operations: A Concept for the Evolution of Full-Dimensional Operations for the Strategic Army of the Early Twenty-First Century*, Fort Monroe, Va., TRADOC Pamphlet 525-5, 1994.

[11] TRADOC, 1994, p. 1-5.

[12] TRADOC, 1994, p. 1-5.

result in military units being able to decide and act at a tempo enemies simply cannot equal."[13]

According to TRADOC, the RMA would be particularly significant with regard to battle command, how units operate together, and how they integrate into a larger whole.[14] Armies would have to organize differently and become more dispersed and nonhierarchical; commanders would have to command differently. The battlefield, moreover, would become "empty" as armies substitute "situational knowledge for traditional physical control."[15] TRADOC also enthused that the battlespace would become "extended," with "an increase in the depth, breadth, and height of the battlefield."[16] Formations would be more "dispersed," and commanders would "seek to avoid linear actions, close-in combat, stable fronts, and long operational pauses."[17]

Another key aspect of future warfare, according to TRADOC, was its "simultaneity." RMA, TRADOC speculated, "may transform the familiar form and structure of military campaigns as a chain of sequentially phased operations."[18] The pamphlet continues,

> Advanced forces will possess the capability to achieve multiple operational objectives nearly simultaneously throughout a theater of operations. This simultaneity, coupled with the pervasive influence of near-real-time military and public communications, will blur and compress the traditional divisions between strategic, operational, and tactical levels of war.[19]

TRADOC offered some other ideas about RMA, but what stands out is the conviction that it was not enough for the post–Cold War Army to think about where and against whom its next fight might be. The Army would have to completely remake itself, or *transform*, to use a term that, although not present in Pamphlet 525-5, would have broader use in the coming years.

The Army spent the remainder of the 1990s engaged in a large-scale effort to reinvent itself for the sake of realizing the revolution by means of modeling, simulations, and wargames. Such programs as Army After Next (AAN) and Strike Force represent steps in this process. Underpinning these efforts were several assumptions, among them the belief in the need to fundamentally reinvent how the Army organizes itself and fights, and the idea that information offsets mass. There was something else the

---

[13] TRADOC, 1994, p. 1-5.

[14] TRADOC, 1994, p. 2-8.

[15] TRADOC, 1994, p. 2-8.

[16] TRADOC, 1994, p. 2-9.

[17] TRADOC, 1994, p. 2–9.

[18] TRADOC, 1994, p. 2-9.

[19] TRADOC, 1994, p. 2-9.

Army was after: Its inability to deploy anything heavier than the 82nd Airborne Division to the Gulf in reaction to Iraq's invasion of Kuwait convinced Army leaders of the need to create a force that ideally retained the lethality of the Army's heavier units but was light enough for rapid deployment. The Army hoped that information technology might obviate the need for armor—greater situational awareness plus maneuverability would yield survivability. It also hoped that such a force would have lighter logistical requirements, which would translate into a smaller and more deployable overall force. In 1999, the Army's belief in the need for a lighter and more deployable force received a boost from criticism generated by Task Force Hawk. This was an effort to deploy Apache helicopters to Albania for operations in Kosovo. The idea was straightforward enough, but the Army proved incapable of sending anything shy of a large, heavy force even if only to operate and protect helicopters, and the deployment took a long time. Rightly or wrongly, Task Force Hawk proved to critics of the Army that it was too heavy and too slow.[20]

Transformation

A major landmark for the Army's pursuit of networked warfare came on October 12, 1999, when the new Chief of Staff of the Army, GEN Eric Shinseki, addressed the Association of the United States Army convention and announced that Army "transformation" would be his priority.[21] Shinseki's vision—or, rather, the new Army vision—was no different than Force XXI, except in its greater ambition.

Shinseki envisioned three types of forces that would lead the Army's transformation. First, there would be the "legacy force," or the existing heavy forces. Second would be the "interim force," which would be a running experiment, a force that exists in the here and now but incorporates to the greatest extent possible new technologies, new doctrines, and more. Among other things, the interim force was not to be a division, as in Force XXI or Division XXI, but rather a modular brigade as envisioned by Douglas Macgregor in *Breaking the Phalanx*.[22] It would also be a lighter force than anything currently in the Army and would make heavy use of off-the-shelf equipment, an idea that led to the Army's adaptation of a variant of the Canadian Light Armored Vehicle, which became the Stryker. Shinseki wanted the interim force to be operational by 2010. Third would be the "objective force," which would be the climax of RMA in

---

[20] Adams, 2008, pp. 54–61; John Sloan Brown, *Kevlar Legions: The Transformation of the U.S. Army, 1989–2005*, Washington, D.C.: United States Army Center for Military History, 2011, pp. 170–171; Bruce R. Nardulli, Walter L. Perry, Bruce R. Pirnie, John Gordon IV, and John G. McGinn, *Disjointed War: Military Operations in Kosovo, 1999*, Santa Monica, Calif.: RAND Corporation, MR-1406-A, 2002.

[21] Eric K. Shinseki, address during the Eisenhower Luncheon of the 45th Annual Meeting of the Association of the United States Army, Washington, D.C., October 12, 1999.

[22] Douglas A. Macgregor, *Breaking the Phalanx: A New Design for Landpower in the 21st Century*, Westport, Conn.: Greenwood Publishing Group, 1997.

the Army and embody everything aspired to by the AAN and more.[23] Shinseki, moreover, wanted to be able to deploy an objective force brigade in four days, a full division in five, and five divisions in 30 days.[24] The objective force also would consist of an entirely new suite of networked information systems, sensors, and 18 vehicle types, known as Future Combat Systems (FCS).

Network-Centric Warfare

As discussed earlier, the term *network-centric warfare* originates with VADM Cebrowski and Garstka, who in January 1998 published "Network-Centric Warfare: Its Origin and Future," in *Proceedings*. In their article, they argued that "we are in the midst of a revolution in military affairs (RMA) unlike any seen since the Napoleonic Age, when France transformed warfare with the concept of *levée en masse*."[25]

Consistent with the idea of RMA, advocates insisted that NCW was about more than just a communications architecture. To them, NCW would shape how militaries organized and fought. Thus, in 2000, David S. Alberts, John J. Garstka, and Frederick P. Stein defined *NCW* as

> an information superiority-enabled concept of operations that generates increased combat power by networking sensors, decision makers, and shooters to achieve shared awareness, increased speed of command, higher tempo of operations, greater lethality, increased survivability, and a degree of self-synchronization.[26]

NCW relies on linking traditionally separate streams of information or grids—sensors (which collect the information), decisionmakers (who give the orders), and shooters (who engage the target)—into one coherent superstructure.[27] This allows units to share information horizontally and no longer requires the same hierarchical decisionmaking structure that militaries have relied on in the past. This flatter organizational model, in turn, produces a host of benefits—including enhanced situational

---

[23] TRADOC Military History Office, *TRADOC Annual Command History 1999–2000*, Fort Eustis, Va.: United States Army Training and Doctrine Command, 2006, p. 43; Stuart Johnson, John E. Peters, Karin E. Kitchens, Aaron L. Martin, and Jordan R. Fischbach, *A Review of the Army's Modular Force Structure*, Santa Monica, Calif.: RAND Corporation, TR-927-2-OSD, 2012, p. 10.

[24] Andrew Feickert, *The Army's Future Combat System (FCS): Background and Issues for Congress*, Washington, D.C.: Congressional Research Service, RL32888, April 28, 2005, p. 2.

[25] Cebrowski and Garstka, 1998, p. 1.

[26] David S. Alberts, John J. Garstka, and Frederick P. Stein, *Network Centric Warfare: Developing and Leveraging Information Superiority*, 2nd ed., Washington, D.C.: C4ISR Cooperative Research Program, 2000, p. 2.

[27] Paul Murdock, "Principles of War on the Network-Centric Battlefield: Mass and Economy of Force," *Parameters*, Vol. 32, No. 1, Spring 2002, pp. 90–91.

awareness, more-agile decisionmaking, and generally faster, more-effective military operations.[28]

NCW also was an attempt to answer a growing strategic problem—specifically, the need for decisionmakers to be able to respond faster, particularly in an era of 24/7 media coverage. As Alberts, Garstka, and Stein note:

> A major effect of the fishbowl environment of the Information Age is its effect on the amount of time we have to make a decision. Highly placed decision makers around the globe have noted the greatly increased pressures upon them to react quickly to breaking events, often first finding out about these potential crises, not from their traditional sources, but from the news media. It is ironic that the Information Age, which on one hand gives us vastly increased capabilities to collect and process data that make it possible to make better and better decisions more and more quickly, is—with the other hand—reducing the time available to make decisions. Thus, the race is on. We need to either find ways to respond more quickly with quality decisions, or to find ways to extend the time for critical decisions by expediting other parts of the process.[29]

Networked warfare offered a solution to the problem of compressed timelines for decisions. Thanks to better information-sharing, militaries could move away from rigid hierarchies once needed to mitigate the fog and friction of war and adopt flatter, more-agile organizational structures.[30]

The Promise of Network-Centric Warfare

Part of the reason for NCW's popularity in U.S. military circles was its promised dramatic benefits. To begin with, NCW promised to simplify command and control, speeding up the pace of military operations. By sharing information horizontally—rather than waiting for information to go up and down the chain of command—"network centric warfare enables forces to organize from the bottom up—or to self-synchronize—to meet the commander's intent."[31] Self-synchronization could not only simplify command and control and shorten planning timelines but also could allow forces to react more quickly and with more agility than in previous eras. [32]

Second, NCW also promised to reduce—or at least transform—the military's need for *mass*, or sheer numbers and firepower in military operations. As Erik Dahl

---

[28] Clay Wilson, *Network Centric Operations: Background and Oversight Issues for Congress*, Washington, D.C.: Congressional Research Service, RL32411, March 15, 2007, pp. 2–3.

[29] Alberts, Garstka, and Stein, 2000, p. 65.

[30] Alberts, Garstka, and Stein, 2000.

[31] Cebrowski and Garstka, 1998, p. 1.

[32] Alberts, Garstka, and Stein, 2000, pp. 175–176; Cebrowski and Garstka, 1998, p. 1.

notes, "[m]ass may be the principle of war most challenged by the concepts of NCW."[33] NCW proponents argued that the increasing ability to share information between sensors and shooters coupled with long-range strike meant that the military no longer needed to mass forces at a single point on the battlefield. Rather, the military could operate in a more geographically dispersed manner in what Paul Murdock termed "dispersed mass."[34] Not only was massing forces unnecessary, it was dangerous. Massing forces in this environment would simply make a larger target for the enemy.[35]

Third, and partly because mass was no longer necessary, militaries could employ assets more efficiently and military operations could become cheaper.[36] Because of a better ability to share data across platforms, "smaller, cheaper, more numerous sensors" could be netted together to help "achieve near-real-time surveillance over vast areas."[37] Sensors no longer had to be coupled with the weapon systems, allowing for cheaper munitions because they did not have to be equipped with expensive guidance packages.[38] Moreover, the same platform could perform multiple tasks simultaneously. For example, the same *Arleigh Burke* missile destroyer could perform multiple missions simultaneously, such as protecting a carrier strike group while providing fire support to land forces.[39] Finally, sustainment costs would decrease: Militaries would no longer need to deploy large expeditionary forces and could more precisely forecast their logistical requirements because of better data-sharing and predictive analysis, thereby reducing the cost of the tail of military operations.[40]

Fourth, NCW offered the potential to economize on the amount of damage inflicted on an adversary. Indeed, proponents of NCW often talked about the ability to move from "attrition warfare" to "shock and awe."[41] Because friendly forces had more access to information and could deliver battlefield effects more precisely, they no longer needed to obliterate the entirety of an adversary's forces (i.e., through attrition warfare) to win. Rather, friendly forces could target "significant numbers of critical targets within a short period of time and/or [successfully target] the right target at the

---

[33] Erik J. Dahl, "Network Centric Warfare and the Death of Operational Art," *Defence Studies*, Vol. 2, No. 1, 2002, p. 14.

[34] Murdock, 2002, p. 91.

[35] Murdock, 2002, p. 92.

[36] Murdock, 2002, p. 86.

[37] Edward A. Smith, Jr., "Network-Centric Warfare: What's the Point?" *Naval War College Review*, Vol. 54, No. 1, Winter 2001, pp. 59–60.

[38] Smith, 2001, p. 60.

[39] Murdock, 2002, p. 93.

[40] Wilson, 2007, p. 5.

[41] Alberts, Garstka, and Stein, 2000, p. 184.

right time."[42] Adversaries would experience *lockout*, i.e., friendly forces would operate so fast and so precisely that "one's adversary [would have] no remaining viable courses of action."[43] Friendly forces would be able to detect and neutralize any potential adversary's response, so the adversary could no longer act coherently.[44] Ultimately, locking out adversaries would allow networked forces to reduce collateral damage, minimize casualties, and ultimately shorten the duration of campaigns.[45]

Importantly, not everyone in U.S. military circles bought into NCW's promises. Some felt that it was too expensive or impractical given the limitations on distance, interoperability, and bandwidth.[46] Others felt that such concepts as strategic lockout were far-fetched attempts to find a panacea to warfighting that rarely materialized. As Naval War College professor Thomas Barnett argued, "Ever since Giulio Douhet's *Command of the Air* (1921), we have heard that massed effects against an enemy's centers of gravity can lead swiftly to bloodless victory. And every war since then has seen this theory's vigorous application and subsequent refutation. Yet the notion persists and now finds new life in network-centric's 'lock-out' strategy."[47] Despite this skepticism, NCW's prominence in U.S. strategic thinking continued to grow throughout the late 1990s and the early 2000s.

Rumsfeld's Transformation

The zenith of NCW in U.S. defense strategy came with Secretary of Defense Rumsfeld. Rumsfeld came into office with a vision of transforming the way the U.S. military operated, and President George W. Bush had campaigned on a platform of transforming the military. Although Bush did not mention NCW by name, he had advocated for many of its underlying tenets. In a major speech at the Citadel on September 23, 1999, Bush argued that "power is increasingly defined, not by mass or size, but by mobility and swiftness. Influence is measured in information, safety is gained in stealth, and force is projected on the long arc of precision-guided weapons."[48] Rumsfeld shared Bush's vision, and when he became Secretary of Defense, he tried to make this vision a reality.

Based on the concepts in NCW, Rumsfeld envisioned a lighter, more agile, more networked force. He argued that "the United States must work to build up its

---

[42] Alberts, Garstka, and Stein, 2000, p. 184.

[43] Dahl, 2002, p. 17.

[44] Smith, 2001, p. 64.

[45] Alberts, Garstka, and Stein, 2000, p. 184.

[46] Wilson, 2007, pp. 14, 17–18, 26.

[47] Thomas P. M. Barnett, "The Seven Deadly Sins of Network-Centric Warfare," *Proceedings*, Vol. 125, No. 1, January 1999, pp. 36–39.

[48] George W. Bush, "A Period of Consequences," speech delivered at the Citadel, Military College of South Carolina, September 23, 1999.

own areas of advantage, such as our ability to project military power over long distances, our precision-strike weapons, and our space, intelligence, and undersea warfare capabilities."[49] U.S. combat power would come from being able to rapidly link shooter, sensor, and decisionmakers together to deliver precise effects at great distances. At the same time, like some NCW proponents, Rumsfeld was skeptical of the continued need for mass on the modern battlefield, stating that "the country no longer needs a massive, heavy force to repel a Soviet tank invasion."[50]

The early phases of the Afghanistan and Iraq Wars seemingly validated NCW and Rumsfeld's drive toward an alternative force. According to former special assistant to Rumsfeld John Luddy, "U.S. forces in both conflicts used networked information to achieve huge efficiencies in combat."[51] During the opening phases of the Iraq War, U.S. forces used about 30 times the bandwidth they had employed during the first Gulf War a dozen years earlier.[52] Satellite and unmanned aerial vehicle imagery was pushed down to the brigade level at first and to even lower levels over the course of the war.[53] NCW advocates thought they saw evidence that, thanks to these advancements, the U.S. military did not need to rely on mass in the same way it had done in earlier wars. As Luddy remarked, "In Afghanistan, the deployment of American ground troops was minimal; in Iraq, a force one-quarter the size of the 1991 Desert Storm coalition defeated the Iraqi regime in 21 days, with only 161 troops killed in action."[54]

Both wars produced vivid images of NCW in practice. To Rumsfeld, the iconic image of the horseback riding Special Forces soldier calling in precision airstrikes in Afghanistan captured the essence of NCW and the promise of the RMA.[55] There reportedly were other powerful demonstrations of NCW during the early part of the Iraq War. When U.S. forces ran into a sandstorm during the invasion from March 25–28, 2003, according to one source, the air campaign continued unabated, while Blue Force Tracker (BFT)—a system that digitally depicted all friendly ground units' location—prevented friendly fire incidents on the ground.[56]

The early phases of the Afghanistan and Iraq Wars stopped short of validating NCW. Arguably, neither campaign confirmed the shock and awe and lockout premises of the theory. Despite the fact that the United States referred to the air campaign at

---

[49] Donald H. Rumsfeld, "Transforming the Military," *Foreign Affairs*, Vol. 81, No. 3, May/June 2002, p. 25.

[50] Rumsfeld, 2002, p. 28.

[51] John Luddy, *The Challenge and Promise of Network-Centric Warfare*, Arlington, Va.: Lexington Institute, 2005, p. 3.

[52] Luddy, 2005, p. 25.

[53] Luddy, 2005, p. 25.

[54] Luddy, 2005, p. 3.

[55] Rumsfeld, 2002, p. 21.

[56] Luddy, 2005, p. 9.

the outset of the Iraq War as "shock and awe," the campaign did not kill Iraqi dictator Saddam Hussein or render the Iraqi militaries incapable of mounting a response.[57] Moreover, as many skeptics of NCW noted, Iraq and Afghanistan were at best third-tier adversaries, so the U.S. military's stellar performance in these conflicts (at least initially) may not be generalizable to more-advanced adversaries.[58] Nonetheless, when Bush returned to the Citadel on December 12, 2001, he trumpeted the triumph of NCW, stating that Afghanistan had been a successful "proving ground for this new approach" and that "our commanders are gaining a real-time picture of the entire battlefield, and are able to get targeting information from sensor to shooter almost instantly."[59]

Decline of the Concept in U.S. Military Circles

As the wars in Iraq and Afghanistan dragged on and evolved into their counterinsurgency phases during the mid-2000s, NCW began to go out of style in U.S. military strategic lexicon. As Luddy remarked, "Current operations in Iraq illustrate that efficient, lethal light and medium forces may kill targets and topple an enemy, but securing a peaceful outcome—the war's strategic objective—requires the presence of ordinary troops and heavy armor."[60] Arguably, the same lesson is true of Afghanistan. For all of NCW's focus on improving intelligence collection and communications, information-sharing alone—while valuable—could not accomplish one of the principle imperatives of counterinsurgency: securing the population.[61] Unsurprisingly then, in both Iraq and Afghanistan, the U.S. military needed to return to principles of relying on mass—raw numbers of troops—to accomplish the task.

The U.S. military—and the U.S. Army in particular—also shifted away from NCW programmatically. Most notably, DoD slowed and then canceled FCS after spending an estimated $20 billion on it. Among the problems associated with FCS was that the Army had embraced the idea that better information and communications would obviate the need for armor. However, ongoing military operations in Afghanistan and Iraq made clear the continued importance of physical features, such as heavy armor and V-shaped hulls, in ensuring survivability on the modern battlefield.[62]

---

[57] "'Shock and Awe' Campaign Underway in Iraq," CNN Student News, March 22, 2003.

[58] Luddy, 2005, p. 4; Wilson, 2007, p. 22.

[59] George W. Bush, "U.S. President George W. Bush Addresses the Corps of Cadets," speech delivered at the Citadel, Military College of South Carolina, December 12, 2001.

[60] Luddy, 2005, p. 12.

[61] In fact, in a direct refutation of NCW's core claims about the ability to trade mass for information, the 2006 *Counterinsurgency Manual* claimed that "successful [counterinsurgency] operations often require a high ratio of security forces to the protected population" (U.S. Department of the Army, *Counterinsurgency*, Washington, D.C., Field Manual 3-24, December 2006, p. 1-2).

[62] For a complete analysis of the FCS program, see Christopher G. Pernin, Elliot Axelband, Jeffrey A. Drezner, Brian Barber Dille, John Gordon IV, Bruce J. Held, K. Scott McMahon, Walter L. Perry, Christopher Rizzi,

Importantly, although the popularity of NCW as a buzzword declined in U.S. military circles, the concept did not vanish entirely. The U.S. military has continued to invest resources in improving communications technology and information-sharing within the force long after the cancellation of FCS. Moreover, among foreign militaries, the operational concept of NCW continues to be a foundational concept. Ultimately, Australia, China, France, Germany, Israel, the United Kingdom, and others developed their own concepts of NCW.[63] Some of these countries continued to pursue the concept long after it fell out of vogue in the United States and implemented it as part of their defense modernization programs. As such, these militaries provide a useful counterpoint to the American experience and as important source for potential lessons learned for future U.S. military modernization efforts.

Research Methodology and Overview of the Report

In this report, we explore how one foreign military—specifically, the French Army—developed its own conception of NCW that is similar to, but also quite different from, the American version. The French Army has been putting those theories into practice since the late 1990s by developing associated technologies and using them in training and deployments, including combat missions. Beginning in 2014, moreover, the French Army embarked on an ambitious modernization program known as SCORPION, which resembles FCS.[64] SCORPION and FCS have several differences, but perhaps the most important is that SCORPION is a success, at least from a programmatic point of view. French industry is delivering the planned vehicles and other systems more or less on time, and the French Army is fielding them.

This report draws from various sources. It uses several secondary sources about the French military modernization effort. It relies on various French military publications, including doctrinal manuals and after-action reviews informed by experience with the technology on training grounds or in the field in Afghanistan and Mali. Perhaps the cornerstone in the empirical foundation of this work, however, comes from a series of first-hand interviews. Over the course of a week and a half, a RAND research team interviewed more than three dozen French Army officers on the Army staff, in the *Section Technique de l'Armée de Terre* (STAT) Army technical section, the cavalry (or armor) school, the signal school, and the Land Forces Command—to get

---

Akhil R. Shah, Peter A. Wilson, and Jerry M. Sollinger, *Lessons from the Army's Future Combat Systems Program*, Santa Monica, Calif.: RAND Corporation, MG-1206-A, 2012.

[63] Wilson, 2007, pp. 28–30.

[64] SCORPION is technically an acronym for *Synergie du Contact Renforcée par le Polyvalence et l'Infovalorisation*. Ideally, what the French want is something they describe with a nearly untranslatable word, *infovalorisation*, which means "getting the full value out of information."

a broad view about how the French military is developing and implementing NCW as part of their modernization approach. Nearly all of these officers, it should be noted, have direct experience with either using the technology or commanding others who are using it in training or during overseas deployments. In addition, to get an outsider perspective, the team interviewed a series of French think tank analysts and journalists.

Building on this empirical foundation, this report recounts how the French Army has approached NCW both in theory and in practice. In Chapter Two, we explore the French Army approach to NCW, why Army officials decided to invest in it, how they hoped it might benefit them, and differences between the French and American approaches. In Chapter Three, we provide an overview of French Army NCW programs and technology. Chapter Four describes the French Army's experience using the technology in the field. Most importantly, it details nine major lessons from the French experience with NCW and how these technologies have affected the French Army on a strategic, operational, tactical, and cultural level. Finally, Chapter Five draws on the preceding chapters and unpacks what the U.S. Army in particular and the Joint Force as a whole should take away from the French Army's experience with NCW and with its modernization effort more broadly.

CHAPTER TWO

The French Conception of Networked Warfare

The French Army's conception of networked warfare dates back to the 1990s and must be understood in the context of the evolution of the French Army, as well as its perceived operational requirements, doctrine, and particular institutional cultural traits. It draws on emerging American concepts and on the French Army's reading of the U.S. experience in Afghanistan and Iraq and in later conflicts in Ukraine and Syria. Moreover, this concept has evolved as the French Army has gained experience developing and fielding the technology. As we shall see, French officials have had strong motives for embracing networked warfare, yet in some important ways, they have thought about it differently from officials in the U.S. military and have pursued it in a more conservative and incremental manner. Fundamentally, the French Army, unlike the U.S. Army, did not proceed with the assumption that a revolution was at hand or assume that it would have to redesign its force and rethink how it fought because of the technology. By the time it committed to developing NCW technology, the French Army already had come to an understanding of how its force would be organized and how it would fight. The value of the technology would be to enable the French Army to do what it was already doing, only better.

Betting on Networked Warfare

Deciding to invest in networked warfare technology was not an obvious choice given the French Army's relative lack of financial resources. To date, the French Army has spent billions of euros on networked warfare technology, not including its new fleet of networked armored vehicles. The CONTACT radio program alone is estimated to have cost €3.2 billion.[1] The price tag for SCORPION, including the vehicles, is com-

---

[1] Laurent Collet-Billon, *Audition de M. Laurent Collet-Billon, délégué général pour l'armement, sur le projet de loi de programmation militaire et le projet de loi de finances pour 2014*, Paris, France: Assemblée Nationale, October 2, 2013.

monly cited as €6.5 billion over 20 years.[2] To give a sense of proportion, France's overall defense budget for 2018—all services included—stands at €32.4 billion annually.[3] Yet the French believed they had no choice.

According to a retired French Army officer who served as liaison officer at the U.S. Army's Armor School at Fort Knox in 1994–1996, the French observed with trepidation the U.S. military's embrace of the technology and its enthusiasm for such concepts as RMA and transformation.[4] He said that it was imperative for the French to keep up with the Americans and hold their own in a coalition. That said, the French feared that the Americans might be heading in a direction France could not afford to follow. In 1999, the French Army conducted a study that looked at whether it was advisable or even possible to follow the American lead with respect to networked warfare and transformation. The study concluded that, if the technology proved as revolutionary as many Americans claimed, it might significantly strengthen the U.S. military's superiority over the French Army, along with over those of the rest of the world, potentially degrading the relevance of France's armed forces. If France wished to remain a valued partner in coalition operations with the U.S. military, the French Army would have to adopt at least enough of the technology to operate with the Americans, notwithstanding the fear that by adopting U.S. technology, officials would have to adopt U.S. norms regarding how to fight, which they did not want to do.[5] One study concluded that France could afford the technology.[6] Whereas the Americans at the time were "going all in," the French Army could follow a cheaper, more incremental approach and develop just enough of the new technology to obtain what was needed from it.

In 2014, when the French Army elected to double down on its gamble on networked warfare technology by investing in the more ambitious SCORPION, which combined the networked warfare technology development program with vehicle modernization, another motive entered the picture. The French Army, according to some sources, understood that by combining the networking technology program with vehicle modernization, it would become more difficult for the government to break it into multiple procurement efforts. Several experts even described SCORPION as the

[2]   Roxane Lauley, "Le programme Scorpion démarre," Enterprise Défense Relations Internationales, November 6, 2014.

[3]   "L'Assemblée adopte le budget de la Défense pour 2018," *Le figaro économie*, November 8, 2017.

[4]   Email correspondence with a senior retired French Army officer, June 26, 2018.

[5]   Gérard Bezacier, "La Transformation," *Doctrine: Revue militaire générale de l'armée de terre française*, No. 1, December 2003, p. 5.

[6]   Philippe Gros, Nicole Vilboux, Anne Kovacs, Frédéric Coste, Michel Klein, and Amélie Malissard, *Du Network-Centric à la Stabilisation: Émergence des "nouveaux" concepts et innovation militaire*, Études de l'IRSEM, Paris, France, No. 6, 2010, pp. 120, 122–123.

Army's aircraft carrier in the sense that one cannot simply buy different parts of a carrier or its component systems separately.[7] It was all or nothing.

Optimizing a Scaled-Back Post–Cold War Army

Of course, the French Army also saw a lot of potential in the technology. To be more precise, officials hoped the technology would help them squeeze as much capability as possible out of a force that was significantly smaller than its Cold War predecessor and they imagined that the technology complemented their general operational approach. These assumptions mark important distinctions between the French and U.S. approaches. The U.S. military began with the assumption that, to get the full value out of networked warfare technology, it would have to completely transform how the force was organized and how it operated. U.S. military officials also looked forward to reducing their force structure thanks to the technology. It would enable the force to be lighter and to do the same job with a smaller number of items (i.e., guns, personnel, vehicles). For the French, the force structure was shrinking no matter what. Moreover, by the end of the 1990s, the French had settled on maintaining an army that operated in a certain way. That force, for example, would be relatively light—not because technology permitted, but because that is what the French chose. The French looked to NCW technology not to provoke or justify a revolution, but simply to help them do what they were already determined to do.

In the 20th century until the end of the Cold War, France effectively had two armies: (1) a large and heavy continental force that relied on conscripts and focused on countering first the German and later the Soviet threat, and (2) a smaller and lighter force geared for operations abroad, above all in France's former colonies. After the Cold War, France chose to end conscription and transition to a smaller professional army. One reason for this transition was purely fiscal: There was a desire to reap a "peace dividend."[8] Another reason was that the old "mixed" force, despite its size, struggled to generate forces for expeditionary operations, largely because conscripts could not be deployed outside of France and Germany. The all-volunteer force France chose would be a primarily expeditionary one and, if anything, the French were giving up their ability to fight the large-scale conventional ground war that defending the homeland against German or Soviet armored divisions once required.[9] Thus, in 1991, the French

---

[7]   Second interview with French Army officers at Centre de Doctrine et d'Enseignement du Commandement in Paris, France, March 8, 2018; Interview with Institut Français des Relations Internationales (IFRI) scholars in Paris, France, March 7, 2018.

[8]   For a detailed account of the 1990s transformation of the French military and the surrounding politics, see Bastien Irondelle, *La réforme des armées en France*, Paris: Presses de Sciences Po, 2011.

[9]   Irondelle, 2011, p. 289.

Army was some 250,000 strong, but struggled to deploy a division (12,000) to participate in the 1990–1991 Gulf War (in comparison, the British Army, with only 160,000 troops, was able to deploy 35,000). To be fair, though, the French also refused to strip their African garrisons, which would have freed up a significant number of deployable professionals.[10] In 1994, the French Army was some 240,000 strong (nine divisions) and 43 percent professional. The *Livre Blanc sur la Défense* of 1994, it should be noted, called for 230,000 personnel to be able to generate a deployable force of 120,000 to 130,000.[11] In 2002, the number was down to 136,000, all professional.[12] The French Army's end strength bottomed out in 2014 with roughly 100,000 (66,000 deployable). However, beginning in 2015 and in response to terrorist attacks at home that greatly increased the demands placed on an already overburdened force, France has been growing its army to reach a target of 77,000 deployable troops. The cuts of the 1990s and the first 14 years of the 2000s also disproportionately affected its heavier, mechanized units (what remained of the continental force). For example, according to one source, in 1997, France had 1,022 fire support pieces (including 397 155mm howitzers and several hundred heavy mortars), but the numbers had dropped to 208 (including 64 CAESAR howitzers, 80 heavy mortars, and 13 Multiple Launch Rocket Systems) by 2012. As of 2019, France has 230 pieces (77 CAESAR howitzers, 140 heavy mortars, and 13 rocket systems).[13]

To optimize the remaining force, the French in 1999—the same year they decided to invest in networked warfare technology—embraced modularity and dissolved army corps and divisions. The French Army replaced them with combined arms brigades and adopted the battalion-sized combined arms task force known as the *Groupement Tactique Interarmes* (GTIA), or Combined Arms Tactical Group, as the basic fighting formation.[14] The French also withdrew their forces from Germany, reflecting the phasing out of its continental focus. The last French regiment stationed in Germany was dissolved in 2014.[15]

In 1999, the French initiated an armored vehicle modernization program that is ongoing, albeit now under the aegis of SCORPION. The primary motivation for the modernization was not to develop any particular capability, but simply to replace an aging vehicle fleet that was becoming increasingly difficult to maintain. That said,

---

[10] Irondelle, 2011, p. 50.

[11] Ministère de la Défense, *Livre Blanc sur la Défense*, Paris: Ministère de la Défense, 1994, pp. 91, 96.

[12] Centre de Doctrine d'Emploi des Forces, *L'Armée de terre française 1978–2015: Bilan des 37 années d'opérations ininterrompue*, Cahiers du RETEX, Paris: Centre de Doctrine d'Emploi de Force, 2015, p. 23.

[13] Personal communication with Elie Tenenbaum, November 22, 2018. See also Elie Tenenbaum, *The Battle Over Fire Support: The CAS Challenge and the Future of Artillery*, Paris: Institut Français des Relations Internationales, 2012.

[14] Centre de Doctrine d'Emploi des Forces, 2015, p. 23.

[15] Centre de Doctrine d'Emploi des Forces, 2015, p. 23.

modernization provided an opportunity to revisit French Army requirements. French Army officials elected to focus on what they described as the "medium segment" of the capability spectrum, with the intention of being able to cover as broad a swathe of operational needs as possible, i.e., heavy enough to deal with high-intensity warfare—although admittedly only to a point, and with the underlying assumption that France is highly unlikely to get into that kind of fight alone—but light enough to be deployable and sustainable, given France's relatively limited logistical capabilities. During France's 2013 intervention in Mali (Operation Serval), for example, France had to rely on a combination of sealift and borrowed or leased strategic airlift to deploy a brigade-sized light-to-medium force within a few weeks. The French only barely managed to sustain that force in the field, assuming considerable risk in the process.[16]

Emblematic of the French focus on the medium segment is France's new infantry fighting vehicle, the armored infantry combat vehicle, or *Véhicule Blindée de Combat d'Infanterie* (VBCI), which entered service in 2008. The VBCI is an eight-wheeled vehicle designed to replace the 1970s-era tracked AMX-10P. The wheels are a boon for expeditionary operations such as Serval, but the vehicle also offers more protection and firepower than the AMX-10P.[17] In other words, the VBCI is better suited for relatively higher-intensity conflicts than the out-of-date AMX-10P (VBCIs are part of France's heavier formations, including the armored task force France deployed to Estonia in 2019.[18] However, thanks to the wheels, the VBCI remains suited for relatively lower-intensity conflicts, making it the embodiment of the sort of compromises represented by the French Army's commitment to the medium segment. The VBCI also sports France's latest networked warfare technology, but it is not built around that technology in the way in which the new Griffon and Jaguar are said to be.

French Army Doctrine and Culture

There are three concepts or elements that are essential to understanding the French approach to networked warfare technology. The first is a romantic streak that marks at least some French officers. This translates into something like a cult of leadership and the idea of the importance of the human in military operations, a trait that they believe distinguishes them from Americans, whom they regard as overly enamored with tech-

---

[16] For a full discussion of Operation Serval, see Michael Shurkin, *France's War in Mali: Lessons for an Expeditionary Army*, Santa Monica, Calif.: RAND Corporation, RR-770-A, 2014.

[17] VBCIs that participated in Serval drove considerable distances under their own power rather than relying on heavy equipment transporters. They won rave reviews for their mobility and firepower, as well as for the fact that they are air-conditioned. French infantry reportedly took turns in the air-conditioned VBCIs to prevent heatstroke.

[18] Embassy of France in the United States, "France and Allies Reinforce Protection Measures in the Baltic Space," January 29, 2019.

nology.[19] The ideal for many is the young officer leading his men in extreme conditions, making daring calls in situations in which reinforcements or even basic support are out of the question. There is, for example, an element of nostalgia for colonial wars and even calamities such as Dien Bien Phu, which the French remember for the valor of the combatants, including many who volunteered to fight even when the outcome was all but decided. French military culture values "audacity," or bold strokes—the *beau geste*.[20] There is a related emphasis on *rusticité*, on one's ability to "rough it" and endure difficult conditions or make do with equipment, numbers, or support that are by any objective standard far from ideal. The French Army prides itself on this ability. During the debates in the 1990s over investing in the NH90 helicopter program, for example, the Army leadership resisted the new helicopter—which was imposed on it for "European and industrial motives"—because they thought the aircraft was too expensive and too technologically sophisticated.[21] All the Army needed, by the leaders' estimation, "was a flying truck," and they thought that the existing helicopters, although old and out of date, still got the job done.[22]

The second element is the combined concept of *subsidiarité* and command by intent, or the French version of mission command. This is the idea of commanding by communicating to subordinate commanders a general intent, but otherwise entrusting them with the responsibility to realize that intent. Implicit in the idea of *subsidiarité* is faith in the critical importance of the commander's judgment in combat. French Army officers claim that, especially in comparison with the U.S. Army, they train their young commanders to think for themselves and even to push back when they judge it appropriate.[23]

Subsidiarité aligns with the third concept, maneuver warfare. In the French case, *maneuver* means that instead of prevailing through attrition (which they cannot afford) or mass (which they lack), the French Army can win battles by seizing and preserving the initiative and making the one move that, like advancing a chess pawn, sets up a chain of events that makes victory all but inevitable. They refer to this as an *effet majeur* (major effect), which French doctrinal writing contrasts with the Clausewitzian "center of gravity." French officers argue that aiming for the enemy's "center of gravity" connotes attacking the enemy at its greatest strength, while *effet majeur* suggests

---

[19] See Vincent Desportes, "Armées: 'Technologisme' ou 'Juste Technologie?'" *Politique étrangère*, No. 2, 2009, pp. 3–6; and Vincent Desportes, *La Dernière Bataille de France: Lettre aux Français qui croient encore être défendus*, Paris: Gallimard, 2015.

[20] Michael Shurkin, "What a 1963 Novel Tells Us About the French Army, Mission Command, and the Romance of the Indochina War," *War on the Rocks*, 2017.

[21] Irondelle, 2011, p. 294.

[22] Irondelle, 2011, p. 294.

[23] According to one officer, *subsidiarité* no longer exists on a strategic or operational level, but it is still the rule for tactical-level operations.

identifying and striking the enemy's weakest point—an approach well suited for a relatively small military like France's, which has to make the most of few resources.[24] Fighting this way, according to the French, requires encouraging leaders at even the lowest echelons to identify and act on opportunities on their own authority without the constraints of centralized command and control. This has the added benefit, one officer noted, of providing resilience within the chain of command.[25]

Maneuver, *subsidiarité*, and the French Army's romantic vision of command combine to create a vision of warfare that relies on junior commanders making quick decisions that yield quick actions, all intended to seize and hold the initiative and bring to bear enough mass and firepower at the right time and place to make a difference, notwithstanding the French Army's relatively small size. As we shall see, the French Army has been interested in networked warfare technology to the extent to which they see it as helping them realize this ideal of warfare, and they are leery of the prospect that it might have the opposite effect.

Initial Expected Gains

Particularly when compared with those of the U.S. military, French aspirations for digitization when they began developing the technology were relatively modest, and they insisted—and still insist—that the technology, rather than revolutionizing French military operations, would enhance their ability to operate as they were already determined to do. It would enable *subsidiarité* and enhance commanders' ability to identify and seize the initiative, and it generally would increase the lethality of the GTIA by making optimal use of the effects of the combined arms that are organic to the GTIA. Networked warfare would help the GTIA be more than the sum of its parts. French officers insist that the idea was never to replace larger formations with smaller ones. The balance of forces and mass still counts; quality can replace quantity only up to a point. Similarly, the French officers insist that they never held out the hope that the technology would obviate the need for armor.[26] In the words of one officer, "the point wasn't to make the force lighter, but to optimize its lethality, to put the fires where it counts, and to employ fires more intelligently."[27] Another way of looking at the matter is that French forces since the mid-1990s were getting lighter as the French Army chose to focus on expeditionary operations while being cognizant of what one could and

---

[24] For a thorough discussion of the idea of *effet majeur*, see Michel Yakovleff, *Tactique Théorique*, 3rd ed., Paris: Economica, 2016. See also *effet majeur* as defined by French Army doctrine in Centre de Doctrine d'Emploi des Forces, *Tactique Générale*, Paris: Armée de Terre, 2008, p. 40.

[25] Personal communication with a French field officer, French Ground Forces Command, December 21, 2018.

[26] Interview with French Army officers at STAT in Versailles, France, March 6, 2018.

[27] Interview with French Army officers at Centre de Doctrine et d'Enseignement du Commandement in Paris, France, March 7, 2018; Interview with SCORPION Battle Lab director in Paris, France, March 8, 2018.

could not do with fewer and lighter vehicles. French officials did not look to networked warfare technology to change that calculus.

Perhaps the most important and enthusiastic early advocate for networked warfare in the French military establishment is General Guy Hubin (ret.), who in 2000 published a book on networked warfare that imagined technology profoundly transforming how wars were fought.[28] Hubin's book is similar to the enthusiastic writings on RMA, and later on transformation, published by Americans in the late 1990s and early 2000s. The book has been widely read in the French Army. For a while it was required reading for students preparing for the entrance exam of the French Army's prestigious École de Guerre, and it remains on the recommended reading list for those who pass that test. All those interviewed for this study were familiar with Hubin's book. However, all agreed that Hubin was an outlier, and that his vision, if it ever becomes reality, is unlikely to do so anytime soon.[29]

Much of Hubin's book would be familiar to readers of comparable American documents, such as the writings on RMA and NCW cited earlier, or *Joint Vision 2020*.[30] He envisioned the technology encouraging the dispersal of forces and their intermingling with the enemy—there will be no more linear fronts. Organizations will become flat: "[T]he performance of modern communications systems will put an end to pyramidal structures and replace them with networked organizations."[31] After all, he argues, with everyone networked, there is no need for information to flow according to any particular hierarchy.[32] Hubin's vision is of mobile units that, because everyone knows exactly where they and their fellows are, can rapidly coordinate precise movements and fires, can quickly take advantage of whatever opportunities arise because they are able to organize and reorganize themselves on the fly, and can disperse and mass forces precisely at the right place and the right time. The forces involved would be highly dispersed, both for reasons of safety (to counter the enemy's ability to concentrate firepower) and because future units will cost so much that a small number will have to control larger areas.[33] According to Hubin, "In the future, taking into account the effectiveness of air/ground indirect fires, any concentration at the level of our current companies will be destroyed even before they are engaged."[34]

---

[28] Guy Hubin, *Perspectives Tactiques*, 3rd ed., Paris: Economica, 2009, p. 176.

[29] Interview with IFRI scholars in Paris, France, March 7, 2018; Interview with French Army officer at the École de Transmissions in Cesson-Sévigné, France, March 13, 2018. Hubin now acknowledges that he overestimated the speed of technological advances and their impact, noting, for example, how little light networked warfare technology sheds on enemy forces (interview with General [ret.] Guy Hubin in Paris, France, March 9, 2018).

[30] Joint Chiefs of Staff, *Joint Vision 2020: America's Military—Preparing for Tomorrow*, Washington, D.C., 2000.

[31] Hubin, 2009, p. 175.

[32] Hubin, 2009, p. 64.

[33] Hubin, 2009, pp. 105–106.

[34] Hubin, 2009, p. 76.

Tactics, according to Hubin, would consist of many small formations maneuvering largely independently, often in different directions, and taking advantage of different opportunities while acting collectively to achieve a shared objective that ideally would not be immediately obvious to the opponent. Keys to success would be speed (of decision and maneuver) and the ability to maintain freedom of action. In an interview for this study, the retired general asserted the importance of accepting risk for the sake of rapid action ("do something wrong but do it quickly").[35] Moreover, in light of a technologically sophisticated opponent's awareness of the movements of one's forces, victory is "not about surprise but rather exploitation of opportunities."[36] Hubin also puts much store in the potential for the new technology to significantly enhance logistical capabilities while reducing the quantity of supplies that armies must move. Future forces will fire far fewer rounds of ammunition, he postulated; they also will receive precisely the parts they need, when and where they need them.[37]

A few things distinguish Hubin's vision of NCW from the American writings on NCW and make it discernably French. First, he insists on a measure of anthropocentrism, of placing the human commander and consumer of information at the center of everything, and not to put everything on the technology. Thus, he caveats his exhortation to embrace networked technology:

> That one must frame the work of engineers and the laboratories in healthy and realistic limits, and avoid the distractions of the "always more," goes without saying. That one must banish the idea that technology can be a substitute for the soldier and detach him from his environment to make of him a sort of "robocop," that is certain. Finally, that one must refuse to give in to the naive temptation consisting of imagining that for every operational problem there necessarily exists a new technological response, is obvious.[38]

Second, Hubin's vision conveniently dovetails with the French Army's emphasis on *subsidiarité* and decentralized command. All of those small formations operating simultaneously, but autonomously, and rapidly reacting to emerging opportunities are acting on their own initiative. Presumably, moreover, these would be lower-echelon units, i.e., platoons, squads, companies, *Sous Groupement Tactique Interarmes* (SGTIAs), and GTIAs. Future fights will not be won by a commanding general perched godlike atop a hierarchy from which he can see the entire front, but rather by some lieutenant or captain, who on his or her own would see a gap and act, thereby achieving the *effet majeur*. The officer, moreover, probably would act with the help of

---

[35] Interview with General (ret.) Guy Hubin in Paris, France, March 9, 2018.

[36] Interview with General (ret.) Guy Hubin in Paris, France, March 9, 2018.

[37] Hubin, 2009, pp. 129–133.

[38] Hubin, 2009, p. 178.

precision fires provided by a few artillery tubes or an aircraft commanded by men or women who communicated with him or her, but not necessarily with their own superiors. In Hubin's writing on the subject, one finds more than a little of the romanticism mentioned above:

> The direction of execution must remain the affair of the young officers and the more solid non-commissioned officers, at the level of our current platoon or company commanders and our young captains. Entirely consumed with serving their weapons and using the terrain, they will put the enthusiasm, vivacity, and the lack of self-consciousness of their youth at the service of the brutality of the action. They will take everything in with a single glance, and, acting with intuition and animated with the desire to win, they will make use of more and more complicated materials, the employ of which will focus their attention, and the mastery of which will have required long training and continual practice. The result will be the destruction of the enemy.[39]

In other words, Hubin sees NCW as playing to the French Army's strengths, or at least what French officers believe to be their strengths. Elsewhere, he states that, in a war against peers with a similar level of technical sophistication, the advantage will be with the side whose young commanders simply do NCW better, meaning those who are better trained and better equipped to make the fullest use of the technology, absorb and synthesize the vast quantities of information in constant flow, discern what to do, and get it done.[40]

It follows that French officers and military publications, when discussing the hoped-for gains of networked warfare technology, consistently cite speeding up U.S. Air Force Col John Boyd's famous OODA Loop.[41] The idea is that the technology would enable French officers to know more and, presumably, identify opportunities faster and move more rapidly to seize them.[42] They insist on the technology's compatibility with or even contribution to *subsidiarité* and maneuver. For example, a 2009 French Army publication on networked warfare states that the technology should make maintaining *subsidiarité* easier.[43] As we shall see, however, some French experts are skeptical about whether the technology fosters *subsidiarité* or, on the contrary, tends to reinforce a latent trend toward centralization.

---

[39] Hubin, 2009, p. 75.

[40] Hubin, 2009, p. 109.

[41] Taylor Pearson, "The Ultimate Guide to the OODA Loop," webpage, undated.

[42] Michel Asencio, *Les opérations en réseau: Vision d'ensemble*, Fondation pour la Recherche Stratégique, No. 3, 2009, p. 4; Martin Klotz, "Les enjeux capacitaires de la numérisation de la NEB," *Doctrine Tactique*, No. 27, June 2013, p. 7.

[43] Centre de Doctrine d'Emploi des Forces, *Principes d'organisation de commandement et d'emploi d'une force numérisée: Utilisation de la numérisation*, Paris: Ministère de la Defense, 2009, p. 30.

The French observed U.S. military operations in Afghanistan and Iraq in the early 2000s with great interest. What they saw validated their theories about what networked warfare might bring. Of particular interest was the U.S. Army's Stryker units, which in many ways pioneered networked warfare operations. A 2005 French Army study noted, for example, that thanks to digitization, U.S. Stryker company commanders had the same perspective that battalion commanders used to have, and Stryker formations could cover three times the geographic area that nondigitized Bradleys could.[44] The document also noted that, because in counterinsurgency campaigns such as Iraq, formations tended to be smaller, so lower-echelon commanders exercised greater *subsidiarité*. The technology helped by freeing the commanders and their deputies from various tasks and giving them a broader situational awareness.[45] The study also asserted that digitized companies in Iraq had a greater ability to coordinate in part because they had access to precise information, with the result that battalions were losing their value and brigade organizations were becoming flatter. Ultimately, what the French saw in the U.S. experience in Iraq was evidence that "in mobile combat, digitized units have on average more time at their disposal than non-digitized units."[46] The units can "better prepare defensive organizations, chose their firing positions, attack an enemy sooner and at a greater distance, and avoid obstacles more easily."[47] The French also saw evidence of real benefits for logistics teams, which now knew precisely where a forward unit was going to be and when and precisely what it needed to be resupplied. This makes it easier to practice just-in-time logistics. Basically, the technology facilitates anything that requires precise coordination between two friendly units, be it logistics, fires, or any other form of support.[48]

Perhaps what impressed the French most about the U.S. use of networked warfare technology in Iraq was BFT, the purported advantages of which they seemed to dwell on more than the U.S. military did.[49] Indeed, as far as the French are concerned, BFT

---

[44] Centre de Doctrine d'Emploi des Forces, *Des electrons et des hommes: Nouvelles technologies de l'information et conduite des opérations*, Cahier de la recherche doctrine, Paris, 2005, p. 17. Subsequent French Army studies picked up on Daniel Gonzales et al.'s work at RAND on the performance of Stryker units in Iraq (see Dan Gonzales, Michael Johnson, Jimmie McEver, Dennis Leedom, Gina Kingston, and Michael S. Tang, *Network-Centric Operations Case Study: The Stryker Brigade Combat Team*, Santa Monica, Calif.: RAND Corporation, MG-267-1-OSD, 2005; and Michel Goya, "Dix ans d'expérience des brigades numérisées Stryker," *Lettre du Retex-Recherche*, No. 16, May 2014).

[45] Centre de Doctrine d'Emploi des Forces, 2005, p. 17.

[46] Centre de Doctrine d'Emploi des Forces, 2005, p. 14.

[47] Centre de Doctrine d'Emploi des Forces, 2005, p. 14.

[48] Centre de Doctrine d'Emploi des Forces, 2005, p. 15.

[49] See, for example, Centre de Doctrine d'Emploi des Forces, 2005, pp. 12, 14, 16–17; Gros et al., 2010, pp. 111–114; Rémy Hémez, *L'Avenir de la surprise tactique à l'heure de la numérisation*, Paris: Institut Français des Relations Internationales, 2016, p. 21; Centre de Doctrine d'Emploi des Forces, "La transformation de 4 forces terrestres alliées: vers un modèle à la française?" *Héraclès*, Vol. 4, 2004, pp. 3–4.

alone is enough to justify investing in networked warfare. Among the advantages they associated with BFT are

- lowered rates of fratricide[50]
- a significantly heightened ability to seize opportunities and maneuver on the battlefield by giving commanders precise and real-time information regarding where their forces are located[51]
- alleviation of the burden of having to constantly figure out where one is and where everyone else is, freeing commanders to focus on other things
- a greater capacity to disperse their forces and concentrate them at the right time and place.

Interestingly, one French officer saw a danger in BFT working too well.[52] He argued that it encourages users to place too much confidence not just in the accuracy of what they see on a display but on the completeness of that information. He suggested that, rather than perfecting BFT by increasing the refresh rate to nearly instant, it might be better to have a relatively lower refresh rate so as to encourage an element of distrust among users.

The most recent articulation of French Army theoretical views on networked warfare is Lieutenant Colonel Rémy Hémez's 2016 *L'Avenir de la surprise tactique à l'heure de la numérisation* [*The Future of Tactical Surprise in the Age of Digitization*], which, although it is more narrowly focused than Hubin's 2000 work, in many ways represents an update to his work. Hémez is interested in the question of whether tactical surprise is even possible, given the heightened situational awareness ostensibly furnished by networked warfare technology. His answer is yes, it is, for several important reasons. One reason is the inevitable incompleteness of the information collected and aggregated by sensors and information systems, a risk that is heightened by the danger that officers looking at the wealth of information on their screens might (1) assume what they see is accurate, (2) confuse what they see with the whole of relevant information, and (3) ignore all the human biases and errors that cannot help but be introduced whenever humans are making decisions about what to report, and how.[53] Another reason why surprise is still possible is that surprise is not only about the unexpected; it also is about actions to which there is too little time to respond. The technology, to the extent that it can speed up an adversary's ability to act, can enhance the risk that

---

[50] Klotz, 2013, p. 7.

[51] Klotz, 2013, p. 7.

[52] Interview with French Army officer at Commandement des Forces Terrestres in Lille, France, March 14, 2018.

[53] Hémez, 2016, pp. 23–24.

one might not be able to respond even to something one anticipates.[54] A third reason is that surprise often is about breaking a rule or otherwise "depart[ing] from a frame of reference" for the sake of "creating shock among the adversary."[55] Ultraviolence, for example, can come as a surprise and shake up an adversary. Also, the embrace of networked warfare technology makes the network itself a target, one that adversaries can target, disrupt, shut down, or spy on, introducing a range of possible unpleasant surprises.[56] Finally, the technology can increase the range of possible actions, particularly as forces disperse and units organize less hierarchically and linearly. This makes it more difficult for an adversary to anticipate an action. One might suspect an attack, but it can be more difficult to anticipate by whom and where the attack will occur if the possibilities are greater. Hémez cites with approval the idea of swarming and the Israeli operations in 2002 in Nablus, where Israeli units made a point of going through walls or attacking from above rather than using streets and doors (which achieved surprise not only by virtue of coming from unexpected directions but also by virtue of breaking a frame of reference).[57]

With this point, Hémez is returning to orthodox French Army thinking about *subsidiarité* and mission command. Pointing to the GTIA and the SGTIA as units of action, Hémez sees the key to optimizing the potential gains of networked warfare technology in terms of reinforcing smaller units' autonomy. Achieving tactical surprise is about enabling small units to be as flexible and responsible as possible. This has to be a feature of unit organization (which has to move away from the linear), as well as of the culture inculcated among young French officers.[58] Part of that flexibility, of course, means maintaining the force's culture of *rusticité*.[59] The force needs to be able to fight on even when its information systems are degraded, jammed, or shut down. However, Hémez acknowledges that *rusticité* comes at a cost, and the investment tends to diminish the advantages of using high-tech systems.

Early French Concerns with Networked Warfare

From the beginning, the French have been skeptical about networked warfare, its limitations, and the potential vulnerabilities they fear it might introduce. They consistently have voiced skepticism regarding the ability of networked technology to lift the fog of

---

[54] Hémez, 2016, pp. 22–24.

[55] Hémez, 2016, p. 26.

[56] Hémez, 2016, p. 24.

[57] Hémez, 2016, p. 40.

[58] Hémez, 2016, pp. 33–42.

[59] Hémez, 2016, p. 35.

war regarding Red Forces. Clearly, the increased ability to share information about the enemy represents a real advantage, but the French have assumed that such information would be highly incomplete and potentially dangerous if commanders mistook the data they saw on their screens as complete. "Where is my information superiority," an officer asked, "if I don't know everything or if some of my information is incorrect?"[60]

The French Army's other concerns have been

- the danger of flooding commanders with too much information
- the danger of encouraging commanders to hesitate for the sake of acquiring still more information[61]
- the risk that commanders would pass information up to higher echelons without doing the mental work of sifting out information that needed to be forwarded
- the danger that commanders would rely too heavily on their computer screens, (1) confusing the information represented with the sum total of reality and (2) forgetting to look around them or, as some officers put it, "fail to stick their head[s] out of vehicle hatches"[62]
- overreliance on technology that could be compromised or tricked—or even be shut down—in a conflict with a sophisticated opponent[63]
- overreliance on technology that, like all technology, fails (the French are familiar with Murphy's Law)[64]
- the possibility that higher-echelon commanders or civilian leaders back in Paris might micromanage field operations.[65]

Concerns about a dependence on technology that could translate into a vulnerability is something that haunts French officers in particular, as they acknowledge that they have had little experience with opponents that possess sophisticated electronic warfare capabilities. They also admit that in all their modeling, simulations, and field experiments, they still have not adequately tested what would happen if the technology were degraded. As for the risk of micromanagement, the response of most of the officers interviewed for this research effort is to refer to the French Army's emphasis on *subsidiarité* and the belief that French Army officers simply would not fall to the

---

[60] Interview with a French Army officer at Commandement des Forces Terrestres in Lille, France, 2018.

[61] Marc Espitalier, "Le chef et la machine," *Fantassins: Le magazine d'information de l'infanterie*, No. 36, 2016, p. 28.

[62] Yves Jacops, "La NEB: limites et plus-values," *Doctrine Tactique*, No. 27, June 2013, p. 11.

[63] Serge Caplain, "Les 10 pièges de la numérisation des forces terrestres," LinkedIn blog, January 15, 2018; Espitalier, 2016, p. 23.

[64] Caplain, 2018. The French generally know the English "Murphy's Law," but they also have their own term, the *loi d'emmerdement maximum* (LEM), which roughly translates to "the law that things will go wrong."

[65] Caplain, 2018.

temptation because it is contrary to their institutional culture and identity. Others were less confident. They argued that, in fact, the principle of *subsidiarité* is already in decline and that French military operations are increasingly centralized, owing at least in part to politicians' relative aversion to risk. Although it is true, one officer explained, that the French still train for decentralized operations, it is becoming less and less of a reality, as more and more actions have to be cleared at higher levels.[66] One officer even laughed when he was told that others were confident that the French culture of *subsidiarité* would enable them to resist the centralizing effect of networked warfare. "Who told you that?" he asked.[67]

Conclusion

The French Army neither designed its NCW technology to address the needs of stability operations or high-end conventional wars per se, nor did it optimize it for any specific region. In the wake of the dramatic post–Cold War draw down, the French Army needed to compensate for its lack of capacity with added capabilities that would apply to as broad a range of scenarios as possible while keeping up with the United States. NCW seemed to offer a solution. By improving information-sharing and overall situational awareness, the smaller French forces could operate more efficiently, accomplishing tasks that previously required larger units. The French did not aim to revolutionize warfare, but rather be better at what they were doing already. As we shall see in the subsequent chapters, this approach has shaped how the French have developed, fielded, and optimized NCW technologies.

---

[66] Interview with French Army officers at Centre de Doctrine et d'Enseignement du Commandement in Paris, France, March 7, 2018.

[67] Interview with French Army officer at the École de Transmissions in Cesson-Sévigné, France, March 13, 2018.

CHAPTER THREE

The French Army's Networked Warfare Program: Systems and Technology

The French today speak of the evolution of their approach and the development of networked warfare technology in terms of two stages. Using the term *digitization of the battle space*, or *numérisation de l'espace de bataille* (NEB), they often refer to the first stage as NEB 1.0 and the second as NEB 2.0. NEB 1.0 refers to the technology that they began to develop and adopt beginning in the 1990s. NEB 1.0 is what the French took to war in Afghanistan and Mali and what one finds today in a French Army unit, whether at home or deployed. NEB 2.0 refers to SCORPION, which includes a massive vehicle modernization program and involves replacing many of the systems that constituted NEB 1.0 with new technology that ostensibly incorporates the lessons learned from the older technology. In this chapter, we discuss the history of the programs associated with NCW and provide an overview of both the NEB 1.0 systems and SCORPION.

One of the hallmarks of the French Army's approach to NCW technology has been its incrementalism. The French have fielded the technology as they have developed it—arguably before it is mature—while striving to derive lessons from the experience that they might apply to future iterations. According to one officer, this is a fundamentally different approach compared with that of the U.S. Army. Americans, he said, prefer mature technology to the point of making the perfect the enemy of the good.[1] The French, in contrast, simply lack the resources to be choosey. They have to field what they develop because they simply cannot afford to walk away from it. Thus, NEB 1.0 represents more than a decade's worth of experimentation. SCORPION, in contrast, represents an effort to apply the lessons of those experiments and replace NEB 1.0 with systems intended to be more mature.

---

[1] Telephone interview with French Army officer at Ecole d'Infanterie, Draguignan, France, May 31, 2018.

Numérisation de l'Espace de Bataille 1.0

Technically, NEB 1.0 predates the French Army's adoption of the idea of networked warfare in 1999. As early as the late 1980s, the French began developing single-purpose systems for applications, specifically for the French Army's nuclear weapon systems (which it gave up in the 1990s) and artillery.[2] In the case of nuclear weapons, the technology had to do with the fact that France's nuclear weapons are under direct political control and not the chain of command; nuclear weapons required a highly secure stand-alone system. As for the artillery systems, according to one French defense expert, a specific motivation was to ensure the efficiency of artillery support given the radical decline of the French Army's artillery resources.[3] Over time, the French developed more systems for more applications and they began connecting those systems using myriad bridges.

More specifically, in the 1990s, the French developed a system known as SICF (*Système d'Information pour le Commandement des Forces*, or Information System for the Force Command) for corps, division, and brigade-level headquarters.[4] The French wanted to link those echelons to lower ones, so they developed SIR (*système d'information régimentaire*, or regimental information system) for battalions and companies. This, too, the French found inadequate, because commanders still had to communicate with soldiers by talking to them on the radio, so they developed the terminal system (SIT) for each platoon leader, tank commander, or others.

The basic elements of NEB 1.0 are therefore SICF, SIR, and SIT (see Figure 3.1). Added to that is a range of different systems generally designed for particular functions or Army branches. For example, FELIN (*Fantassin à Équipement et Liaisons Intégrés*, or Integrated Infantryman Equipment and Communications) links dismounted infantry to one another and to the battalion. Development of FELIN began in 2000. A separate technology networks France's Leclerc main battle tanks. Artillery, logistics, and military intelligence each has its own system.

Most of these systems talk to one another, at least to some degree, although the French make clear that their integration is far from seamless. The bridge connecting SICF and SIR—in other words, connecting the brigade and above on one hand and the regiment and below on the other—often is cited as problematic.[5] Known as SICAT, the bridge between SICF and SIR has a small throughput and can exchange a limited number of messages, which impoverishes communications between brigades

---

[2] Interview with IFRI scholars in Paris, France, March 7, 2018.

[3] Interview with IFRI scholars in Paris, France, March 7, 2018.

[4] Interview with French Army officers at STAT in Versailles, France, March 6, 2018.

[5] Interview with French Army officer at Commandement des Forces Terrestres in Lille, France, March 14, 2018.

and GTIAs.[6] The multiplicity of systems, moreover, has fostered stovepiping, which defeats the purpose of the information network. The French also note complications related to classification, with SIT and SIR operating at the level of the French classification of Mission Restricted (MR), while SICF operates at the higher classification level of Mission Secret (MS). The divide reinforces the general trend of French systems to feed information from the bottom up, but not necessarily in the opposite direction. Moreover, French brigade-level headquarters have both MR and MS systems, which complicate headquarters organization and can create a bottleneck. The French also have different radios for very high frequency (VHF) and high frequency (HF) and other communications gear for different levels. SIR, for example, functions using a Thales digital VHF radio known as *poste radio de quatrième génération* (PR4G), or fourth-generation radio set, which also was developed in the 1990s.

SICF

The French Army deployed its brigade-level and above information system (SICF) in the early 2000s and deployed it for an overseas operation for the first time in 2007 in Côte d'Ivoire. The French have rolled out several versions over the years. Some of the earlier versions were not compatible with SIR. According to the Ministry of Armed

Figure 3.1
Information and Communication Systems of the French Army

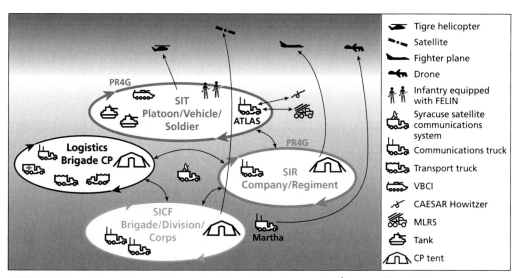

SOURCE: Adapted from Centre de Doctrine d'Emploi des Forces, *Des Électrons dans la brousse: Premiers retours d'expérience de la numérisation de l'espace de bataille*, March 20, 2007, p. 30.
NOTE: CP = command post.

---

[6] Centre de Doctrine d'Emploi des Forces, 2009, p. 7.

Forces, SICF consists of posts that provide "exchange, processing, presentation, storage, and protection services for information necessary to command."[7] SICF further "covers the principal functional domains on the battlefield and takes into account the work of general staff cells such as conception, planning, synthesis, management, intelligence, fire support, logistics and movement," the operating environment, and the "third dimension [i.e., airspace] and electromagnetic spectrum."[8] The system receives and automatically processes information regarding unit situations, threats, orders, and logistical situations, primarily in graphic form on a map; it also allows the command posts using it to coordinate with the other services and with allies, as it is interoperable with the operational information and communication systems of these partners.[9]

SIR

Although it is defined as the French Army's regimental information system, SIR should be thought of as the information backbone of the GTIA and it relies on the PR4G radio and various software applications for specific functions. SIR includes map-based situational displays, "integrated mission planning tools," and coordination and synchronization tools.[10] SIR ostensibly is designed for multinational interoperations because of its compliance with NATO standards and the Multilateral Interoperability Protocol program.[11]

SIR sits between SICF and the various SITEL (*systèmes d'information terminaux élémentaires*), which are the command and information systems used at the operational level, such as ATLAS, the fires coordination system.[12] SIR can be found, for example, on command post variants of such vehicles as the *véhicule de l'avant blindé*, or forward armored vehicle (VAB), and the VBCI. One drawback with SIR is that it operates at a different classification level than SICF does, which hampers the flow of information.[13] SIR reportedly is difficult to use because of its complexity and the different message formats that different subsystems require.[14] The program closed in 2010.[15]

---

[7]   Ministère des Armées, "SICF," webpage, July 4, 2016a.

[8]   Ministère des Armées, 2016a.

[9]   Centre de Doctrine d'Emploi des Forces, *Des électrons dans la brousse: Premiers retours d'expérience de la numérisation de l'espace de bataille*, Cahiers du RETEX, Paris, 2007, p. 38.

[10]   EADS Defense and Security Systems, "SIR (Regimental Information System)," *Defense Update*, No. 3, 2005.

[11]   EADS Defense and Security Systems, 2005.

[12]   Sénat, Projet de loi de finances pour 2012: Défense: équipement des forces, 2011. ATLAS (*l'automatisation des tirs et liaisons de l'artillerie sol/sol*) is a system for the management and automatic transfer of information among regimental groups in their roles involving fires; command; intelligence; logistics; and nuclear, biological, and chemical. For more information, see Ministère des Armées, "Le système ATLAS," webpage, July 13, 2016b.

[13]   Franck Chatelus, "Maîtriser la NEB pour accélérer la décision," *Doctrine Tactique*, No. 27, June 2013, p. 28.

[14]   Centre de Doctrine d'Emploi des Forces, 2007, p. 41.

[15]   Sénat, Projet de loi de finances pour 2013: Défense: équipement des forces, 2012.

SIT

SITs are the information systems used at the levels of tactical execution, such as the company and the platoon. The systems link a unit commander to his or her subordinate echelons, which, in turn, provide data to him or her in a bidirectional exchange. The systems further provide the subordinate echelons with data on their geographic position, the position of allies, detected enemies, and obstacles in their zone of action through a digital map that is shared and updated in near–real time.[16] Among the systems' major advantages are their ability to update information on the tactical and logistical situation, messaging system, and ability to adjust the scale of the map, going from a scale of 1/100,000th to 1/50,000th in just a few seconds.[17]

Multiple types of SIT exist, and each is equipped with different functions based on what kinds of units are using them (see Table 3.1). For example, there is the SITALAT (*système d'information terminal de l'aviation légère de l'armée de Terre*), which is used for the French Army's aviation units, which mostly operate helicopters. It is a Global Positioning System (GPS) tracker with a digital map that can be modified with additional data, such as the position of enemies, infiltration routes, and other strategic elements. As of 2016, it is equipped only on the Army's Gazelle and Cougar helicopters.[18] The Army began experimenting with the system around 2009, when the 3rd Combat Helicopter Regiment received its first aircraft equipped with SITALAT. One of SITALAT's first operational deployments was in 2013 for Operation Atalanta, the European Union–led counterpiracy mission being conducted around the Horn of Africa. It was then used in operations in the Central African Republic, where it allowed users to quickly get sights on objects in urban areas; extract the coordinates of specified objects and transmit them to soldiers on the ground; and determine their positions on digital maps, thereby limiting the risk of friendly fire. Users at the time also noted its resistance to the high temperatures and humidity of the Central African Republic.[19]

Table 3.1
Different Versions of SIT

SIT System	Function
SITALAT	Equipped on light aviation (helicopters)
SIT COMDÉ	Equipped on FELIN soldiers
SIT V1	Equipped on vehicles
SITEL	Equipped on vehicles

---

[16] Centre de Doctrine d'Emploi des Forces, 2007, p. 41.

[17] Centre de Doctrine d'Emploi des Forces, 2007, p. 41.

[18] Ministère des Armées, "La 3D se numérise," webpage, September 5, 2016c.

[19] Frédéric Lert, "Sitalat: les hélicoptères de l'ALAT connectés," *Air & Cosmos*, November 28, 2014.

However, one of the major drawbacks of the system is the difficulty of installing it. In response, the DGA (*Direction générale de l'armement*, or Directorate-General of Armaments) and GAMSTAT (*Groupement aéro mobilité de la section technique de l'armée de Terre*, or Air Mobility Grouping of the Technical Section of the Army) have jointly launched the NUMESIM program.[20] NUMESIM, meaning *numérisation simplifiée*—or simplified digitization—is a program intended to provide French Army helicopters with communication systems that are simpler and easier to equip than SITALAT. Beginning in 2018, the French Army will be able to equip its helicopters with NUMESIM systems, which consist of "a simple box connected by USB cable or Bluetooth to a Getac tablet [a brand of rugged tablets designed by a Taiwan-based company of the same name] equipped with SITALAT software."[21] Although NUMESIM is not as complete as SITALAT, it can be equipped in just a few minutes in place of the PR4G radio box of a helicopter, making it a convenient complement to the full SITALAT.[22]

Another type of SIT is the SIT COMDÉ (*Système d'Information Terminal du COMbattant DÉbarqué*). The SIT COMDÉ serves as the battle management system of FELIN, itself the "digital integrated equipment suite" for dismounted warfighters.[23] According to its creator, the French defense company Safran, it is a touch tablet from which a platoon leader "receives instructions from command units, gives orders and writes reports."[24] The system comprises a "computer and software, a touch pad, [and] a man-machine interface to receive and transmit tactical messages. It allows quick consultation of maps at different scales, real-time geolocation monitoring of different combat groups and consultation of local tactical situations."[25] The system also allows Blue Force Tracking and the transmission of infrared images "acquired by a FELIN-equipped soldier, either from his aiming sight or from JIM infrared binoculars."[26]

Other SITs include the SIT V1, which was deployed in Côte d'Ivoire, and SITEL. SITEL is a vehicle-mounted system made up of a "tactical terminal with touch screen, including a digital mapping function, and an interface with tactical radio, naviga-

---

[20]   The DGA is an agency within the French Ministry of the Armies that is responsible for the design, acquisition, and evaluation of equipment for the French military. GAMSTAT is a testing center specializing in materiel for Army Aviation. For more information, see Préfet de la Drôme, "GAMSTAT–Chabeuil," webpage, February 8, 2013.

[21]   Emmanuel Huberdeau, "Acceleration de la numérisation de l'ALAT," *Air & Cosmos*, December 7, 2017.

[22]   Huberdeau, 2017.

[23]   Safran, "Sagem Signs Major Contract To Upgrade French Army's FELIN Soldier Modernization System," press release, April 3, 2015.

[24]   Safran, "Soldier Modernization," webpage, undated.

[25]   Safran, "Boar's Head Exercise with the British Army: FELIN Makes European Début," press release, April 12, 2012.

[26]   Safran, 2012.

tion, and observation systems."[27] The system "allows units from different Services to exchange formatted messages, calculate the range of a target, consult databases, and share displays of tactical situations," and is also interoperable with FELIN.[28]

Problems with NEB 1.0

One complaint about NEB 1.0 is that the French Army turned to different companies to develop different information systems for use at different tactical levels or for different functions, with relatively little effort made to impose common standards.[29] For example, Thales produced SICF, and EADS made SIR.[30] Finally, several different companies produced the various SITs, although Nexter, working with Matra, is responsible for the basic SIT.[31] The result is a relative lack of interoperability among French Army systems, which is cited as a basic flaw of the technology. One Army publication, for example, notes the lack of "conviviality" between SICF and SIR, and notes that simple mistakes, such as entering data with a special character that works with one system but not another, can throw a wrench into the works, resulting in the loss of information—that neither the sender nor the receiver might be aware of—or in "unsupportable" delays caused by efforts to rectify the problem.[32] Users have to be rigorous in the application of rules that guarantee compatibility when entering data and submitting orders.[33] This also means that users have to devote training time to learning how to use all the different systems and to navigating their particular idiosyncrasies.

Another publication sized up the problem with NEB 1.0 in terms of an "original sin:" NEB 1.0 consists of multiple vertical systems designed for specific functions without the need for them to talk to one another "natively integrated."[34] The result is a "panoply of professional tools that perform well, but rest on technical choices and

---

[27] Safran, "Sagem Receives 500 New Orders for SITEL Tactical Information Systems for French Army," press release, October 6, 2009.

[28] Safran, 2009.

[29] Interview with French Army officers at French Army General Staff in Paris, France, March 9, 2018.

[30] Thales, "Thales proposera le premier système d'information et de commandement interopérable pour l'Armée de Terre et la Marine Française," press release, February 16, 2016; Jean Guisnel, "Le programme Scorpion, ou l'avenir des armements terrestres français," *Le Point*, August 1, 2008.

[31] Le Portail de l'Armement, "NEXTER SYSTEMS," homepage, undated.

[32] Chatelus, 2013, p. 26.

[33] Chatelus, 2013, p. 26.

[34] Eric Cotard, "NEB: de l'adolescence à la maturité," *Doctrine Tactique*, No. 27, June 2013, p. 19.

architectures that are seldom or not at all compatible."[35] There's no "global approach."[36] To the extent that NEB 1.0 works, it is the result of a "federating solution" (here, the author is referring specifically to SICAT) that converts data so that they are understandable by another system. Developing this capability was a "long and fastidious" effort that began with messaging but expanded to other functions."[37] The result is functional, but far from perfect.

Part of that "federating" effort has been creating a common "semantic lexicon," which was developed by the Army staff and ultimately imposed on industry. The objective is a level of coherence referred to as Coherence Level 1, or *Niveau de cohérence 1*, which the French hope to achieve by 2019.[38] The work has been difficult, as the Army staff has to meet the needs of each Service arm. There is also the problem of interoperability: The developers originally focused on French standards only, but later began work to ensure that what they were doing complied with NATO standards.[39] Here, again, classification created headaches. Specifically, the divide in French networks between MS (brigade and above) and MR (battalion and below) was a problem. According to French sources, NATO systems are all MS.[40] In addition to technical problems, there were policy issues. Interoperability compounds the problem by raising questions regarding precisely how much and what kind of information one shares.

Furthermore, the ability to conduct truly collaborative warfare, with platforms automatically sharing information horizontally and vertically, is limited to the Leclerc and the VBCI.[41] According to our sources, that capability will become more generalized throughout the force only when SCORPION is fully in place.

In a sense, NEB 1.0 was NCW more in name than in practice. A host of technical and policy problems with its implementation created obstacles to information-sharing and prevented the French Army from fully realizing the benefits that NCW advocates postulated.

FELIN

The FELIN system, which was made by Sagem, is a suite of personal gear intended to be worn by dismounted infantry. Development of FELIN began in 2001; it entered service in 2010 and was fielded in Afghanistan in 2011.[42]

---

[35] Cotard, 2013, p. 19.

[36] Cotard, 2013, p. 19.

[37] Cotard, 2013, p. 20.

[38] Interview with French Army officers at French Army General Staff in Paris, France, March 9, 2018.

[39] Interview with French Army officers at French Army General Staff in Paris, France, March 9, 2018.

[40] Interview with French Army officers at French Army General Staff in Paris, France, March 9, 2018.

[41] Telephone interview with French Army officer at Ecole d'Infanterie, Draguignan, France, May 31, 2018.

[42] See Land Force, "Mag Terre Vidéo 47," YouTube, May 14, 2011.

Much of the FELIN suite is not related to NCW per se. It includes new optics and night-vision gear, new body armor, a new backpack, etc. Of those, the optics are particularly prized, because they purportedly double the effective accurate range of the French infantryman's standard-issue FAMAS and HK416 rifles (to 600 meters, at least for the FAMAS) and obviate the need to swap out the scope for a separate night-vision device. However, the core of FELIN is a communications system that networks dismounted infantrymen to one another, to their company commander (who is the bridge between the networked infantry and the SIT network used by the VBCI), and to the rest of the regiment. The system includes osteopathic headsets and radios for voice communication, a chat capability, some ability to share photos and video, and the ability to see where everyone is on a small screen, as well as the ability for that information to feed into the commander's battle management software (see the discussion of SIT COMDÉ earlier in this chapter).

VBCI

The VBCI infantry fighting vehicle—a roughly 28-ton 8x8 wheeled vehicle with a 25mm automatic cannon and space to carry nine infantrymen—represents the first major piece of the French Army's vehicle modernization program that subsequently became wrapped up in SCORPION.[43] It deserves mention in the context of NEB 1.0 because, from the beginning, the program promised NCW capabilities. The VBCI comes with a SIT, which allows it to talk to other VBCIs and share data with nearly anyone else within radio range.[44] This permits the use of a battle management system, a cartography system, BFT, and chat, at least among VBCIs. Indeed, VBCIs with the Leclerc share the distinction of being France's only armored vehicles capable of fully collaborative warfare. VBCIs also "talk" to Leclercs, as they were intended to operate together with the tanks in heavy formations.[45] Command variants also have SIR, which links them to the regimental networks and above, and VBCIs can serve as network nodes for FELIN-equipped infantry, making them a bridge between the lowest echelons and higher ones. VBCIs received strong praise for their performance in Afghanistan and Serval, although generally for their mechanical attributes: their mobility, firepower, and the simple fact that they are air-conditioned, which is a must in places like the Sahel. We have found no reports concerning the added value of their NCW capabilities.

---

[43] The VBCI was designed to be just light enough to be transportable by the new A-400M transporter.

[44] Telephone interview with French Army officer at Ecole d'Infanterie, Draguignan, France, May 31, 2018.

[45] Telephone interview with French Army officer at Ecole d'Infanterie, Draguignan, France, May 31, 2018.

SCORPION (NEB 2.0)

SCORPION, which the French Ministry of Defense formally launched in 2014, is both an armored vehicle modernization program and a comprehensive effort to replace the major constituent parts of the various communications and information systems associated with NEB 1.0. The basic idea, besides replacing antiquated and worn-out armored vehicles, is to build on the lessons learned operating NEB 1.0. Most importantly, this will be accomplished by sweeping aside the many different component parts that were developed independently and are said to interoperate together suboptimally. SCORPION will replace the Rube Goldberg–esque tangle of information systems with two systems designed from the beginning to interoperate seamlessly. The other key objective is to radically improve the ergonomics of NEB 1.0 systems— another critical lesson learned. As we discuss in detail in the next chapter, the French believe that one of the major reasons networked warfare technology has not lived up to its potential is because its users—officers and soldiers—simply find it too difficult to use. Ideally, what the French want is something they describe with a nearly untranslatable word, *infovalorisation*, which means getting the full value out of information. The official, doctrinal definition of *infovalorisation* is "the exploitation of the value added by information resources permitted by the new information and communication technologies in order to improve operational effectiveness."[46]

SCORPION has two phases. The first phase consists of introducing two new vehicle families—the *Véhicule blindé multi-roles* (VBMR) multi-role armored vehicle (now known as the Griffon) and the *Engin blindé de reconnaissance et de combat* (EBRC) armored reconnaissance and combat vehicle (now known as the Jaguar; it is essentially a light tank)—along with upgrades for the Leclerc main battle tank.[47] The French also are replacing the PR4G with the CONTACT radio and rolling out the SCORPION Information and Combat System (SICS) and the *Système d'information des armées*, or the Joint Information System (SIA). The plan has been to begin delivering the Griffon and Jaguar in 2018–2021, with the goal of deploying a SCORPION GTIA by 2021 and deploying a SCORPION brigade by 2023. The French Army received its first Griffon in July 2019 and is scheduled to receive its first Jaguars in 2020. The second phase of SCORPION, which is scheduled to take place between 2023 and 2034, will feature initiatives largely intended to strengthen SCORPION and expand its usage throughout the Army. French Army documents more specifically report three domains of activity: (1) expanding SCORPION's use in GTIAs, particularly in terms of completing delivery of the new vehicles; (2) enlarging the capabilities of the GTIA, such as through new engineering vehicles and better exploitation of drones; and (3) consolidat-

46 Caplain, 2018.

47 Direction Générale de l'Armament, "Le ministère de la Défense commande les premiers véhicules blindés GRIFFON et JAGUAR du programme SCORPION," press release, April 22, 2017.

ing *infovalorisation* by distributing the latest information and communication technologies beyond the GTIA level. In terms of equipment, Phase 2 of the SCORPION program will include upgrading the VBCI and introducing new vehicles, such as the light Armored Assistance and Engagement Vehicle (*véhicule blindé d'aide à l'engagement*, or VBAE) to replace light armored vehicles and the Contact Support Medium (*moyen d'appui au contact*, or MAC) to replace the Armored Engineer Vehicle (*engin blindé du genie*). The French also intend to replace FELIN and pursue robotization.

In the following sections, we provide an overview of basic components of SCORPION before focusing on two specific capabilities that SCORPION ostensibly will bring: what the French describe as "collaborative protection" and "embarked simulation."

SICS and SIA

The SCORPION program will replace with SICS all the various command information systems from SIR at the brigade level down to the squad level except for ATLAS, which, according to one source, was left independent to avoid burdening the network with large quantities of data irrelevant to most units.[48] SIA is joint and is intended for the corps and division levels. It will be common to, or at least connected with, the French Air Force and French Navy, giving the three Services a common command and control system across the Services (see Table 3.2).[49]

The French Army envisions equipping all vehicles with SICS starting as early as 2018. SICS will serve as the sole command information system for units from the regiment level down, whether operating as a GTIA or an SGTIA, replacing such systems as SIR and SIT. Later editions of the SICS also will incorporate current FELIN applications.

Table 3.2
Conceptualization of the Evolution of French Command Information Systems

Current	SCORPION	Level Used
SICF	SIA	Corps
		Division
SIR/SIT (SITALAT, SIT COMDÉ, SITEL, and others)	SICS	Regiment
		Battalion
		Company Platoon Squad

SOURCE: Interview with French Army officers at STAT in Versailles, France, March 6, 2018.

---

[48] Personnel communication with Elie Tenenbaum, November 22, 2018.

[49] Thales, 2016.

SICS will have two interfaces. The interface for GTIA command posts and company commanders will be similar to the office automation technology available to civilians, while the one for dismounted company, platoon, and section commanders will have a touch screen and be similar to a tablet or smartphone. SICS will have different versions with functions suited to infantry combat, intelligence collection, and special forces operations.[50] The overall goal is to integrate all forces on all platforms. According to one report, "SICS will . . . achieve an unprecedented integration of combined arm components into a global and digitized whole: FELIN infantry, CAESAR cannon, Leclerc tank, Tigre helicopter, VBCI, VBMR, EBRC, drones. Everyone will see the same thing at the same time."[51]

CONTACT

Another key element of SCORPION is Thales' not-yet-fielded CONTACT radio, which will replace several systems, most notably the PR4G radio that is currently in service. CONTACT, a software-defined radio, will have significantly greater bandwidth than the PR4G—enough to be able to transmit voice and data at the same time, handle BFT and chat, and share video feeds with those within range (i.e., drone feeds).[52] Although the radio will operate primarily on VHF, it will be able to handle multiple frequency types and is designed to switch frequencies automatically depending on availability and strength.[53] In particular, the radio can communicate with the French Army's Syracuse satellite communications system, which is crucial for such operations as those in the Sahel, which are spread out over large geographic areas.[54] CONTACT also will be compatible with PR4G radios and with the U.S. wave-form standard Auxiliary Communications Service radio.

According to several French defense experts interviewed for this study, CONTACT was not originally seen as a requirement for SCORPION, in part because PR4G works well and is adequate for most purposes. One expert suggested that CONTACT made it onto the Army's must-have list because of lobbying from Thales.[55] In any case, CONTACT's greater capacity compared with that of the PR4G means that it will likely serve the French Army's future needs better than the PR4G.

---

[50] Nicolas Chaligne, "Le système d'information du combat SCORPION," *Fantassins*, No. 36, 2016, pp. 48–49.

[51] Michel Cabirol, "Défense: Cassidian n'a pas vu arriver Bull-dozer," *La Tribune*, April 19, 2013.

[52] Interview with French Army officers at French Army General Staff in Paris, France, March 9, 2018.

[53] Interview with French Army officers at French Army General Staff in Paris, France, March 9, 2018.

[54] Interview with French Army officers at French Army General Staff in Paris, France, March 9, 2018.

[55] Interview with Foundation for Strategic Research and Défense and Sécurité Internationale scholars in Paris, France, March 9, 2018.

VBMR, EBRC, and Upgraded Leclerc

Of course, the most visible part of SCORPION will be France's new armored vehicles, the VBMR (Griffon) and EBRC (Jaguar), which the French are introducing while providing updates to the Leclerc main battle tank to extend its service life. Among other things, the three vehicles will share suites of acoustic and optical sensors and the latest SCORPION-grade CONTACT radio and battle management software.[56] CONTACT will be integrated with another Thales product: Antares. Antares will sit on the roof of the vehicles, will provide "360-degree images around the vehicle," and can detect range-finding and targeting lasers pointed at it.[57] Antares ostensibly will be able to locate the source of the laser and identify, for example, if it came from dismounted infantry, a tank, or some kind of aircraft. It will use algorithms and vetronics to generate and present response options to the crew. Meanwhile, via CONTACT, the system will automatically share data with everyone present with the premise that either the system or others on the network will identify who is best placed to take a shot at the threat, if desired.[58]

The VBMR armored personnel carrier is intended to replace the venerable VAB and its many variants, and the manufacturer, Nexter, began delivering the first Griffon to the French Army in July 2019.[59] According to the Ministry of the Armies, the Griffon "is a 6x6 armored vehicle of around 25 tons, equipped with a remote-controlled turret. It will be available in several versions (troop transportation, command post, observation for artillery and medical evacuation)."[60] See Figure 3.2 for a model of the Griffon. The turret will mount either a .30 or .50 caliber machine gun or a 40mm automatic grenade launcher. The VBMR also will be equipped with the CONTACT radio, which will allow the simultaneous and secure transmission of both voice and data.[61] The main function of the vehicle will be to transport eight infantrymen into combat zones. It will be available in 15 versions, the five main versions of which will be troop transportation, medical, command, artillery observation, and recovery.[62] As of February 2018, the French Armed Forces Ministry's order for the Griffon stood at 936 vehicles.

---

[56] Olivier Hertel, "14 juillet: le Griffon, nouveau blindé high-tech de l'Armée de terre," *Sciences et Avenir*, July 14, 2017.

[57] Hertel, 2017.

[58] Hertel, 2017; Andrew White, "Thales Readies Antares for French Army," *Jane's International Defence Review*, February 14, 2018.

[59] Pierre Petit, "Griffon et Jaguar au cœur de SCORPION," Defense24.news, February 20, 2018.

[60] Ministère des Armées, "Scorpion: Commande des premiers véhicules blindés VBMR et EBRC," webpage, July 5, 2017.

[61] Ministère des Armées, "Lancement du programme CONTACT de radio logicielle," webpage, April 20, 2012.

[62] Petit, 2018.

Figure 3.2
Model of the Griffon

SOURCE: Ministère des Armées, 2017.

In addition to the heavy Griffon, the French Army is developing a light variant of the VBMR known as the Serval. The vehicle's name deliberately conjures the kind of mobile tactics and expeditionary skills the French Army showed in Operation Serval, its 2013–2014 intervention in Mali. On February 12, 2018, Minister of the Armies Florence Parly signed a contract giving this project to Nexter and Texelis. The light VBMR will be 4x4, weigh 15 tons, and be able to carry up to ten soldiers equipped with FELIN systems. It will have the same equipment that other SCORPION vehicles have, including a machine gun remotely operated from the cockpit, threat detectors, and SICS. It will have four primary versions: patrolling, intelligence and reconnaissance, communications relay, and electronic warfare. The French Ministry of the Armies described the Serval as the necessary complement to the regular VBMR, which is a heavy vehicle, and the EBRC, which is a medium-weight vehicle. The Serval will replace a portion of the VABs, or armored personnel carriers. The first deliveries of the patrol version—the model of reference—are scheduled for 2022.[63] The five-year defense budget law passed in June 2018 endorsed buying 978 Serval vehicles.[64]

The EBRC Jaguar is a 6x6, 25-ton vehicle "intended to replace the AMX10RC and Sagaie light tanks, as well as the VABs equipped with Hot missiles. It will be equipped

---

[63] Ministère des Armées, "CP_Developpement du véhicule blindé multi-rôles léger," February 12, 2018.

[64] Pierre Tran, "Meet Serval, France's Next Multi-Role Armoured Vehicle," *DefenseNews*, June 12, 2018.

Figure 3.3
Model of the Jaguar

SOURCE: Ministère des Armées, 2017.

with a telescoped 40mm gun, the MMP medium-range missile, and a remotely operated turret."[65] See Figure 3.3 for a model of the Jaguar. The Jaguar ostensibly will be
able to engage both infantry combat vehicles and reconnaissance vehicles in addition to
modern tanks, particularly in urban zones. As such, it will be able to provide both the
Leclerc and the Griffon with a support and maneuver capability in all probable zones
of engagement.[66] In terms of protection, it should be evolutionary in order to adapt to
"the continuum of operations: intervention, stabilization and normalization. As such,
the protection of the Jaguar should be adapted to crowd control missions as well as to
high-intensity combat in open or compartmented terrains and in urban zones."[67] The
Jaguar is expected to enter service in 2020; the French Army's order stands at 150.[68]

---

[65] Ministère des Armées, 2017.

[66] Petit, 2018.

[67] Petit, 2018.

[68] Jean-François Vaizand, "La minsitre des Armées chez Nexter pour une nouvelle commande," *L'Essor*, February 15, 2018.

The VBMR and the EBRC ostensibly will have in common "70 percent of their components, which will facilitate maintenance operations and logistical maneuver."[69] Thales will be developing both the VBMR and EBRC vehicle electronics—or vetronics—architecture. The vetronics network will integrate the CONTACT radio program.[70] Both vehicles also will have an operating range of 800 km over 72 hours.[71] Both vehicles should further be more mobile than their predecessors and can be transported via air by the Airbus A400M.[72]

Finally, the SCORPION program looks to upgrade the Leclerc tank. These upgrades include specific interfaces for the CONTACT radio system and SICS, as well as a specific armor kit that will allow it to deal with new threats, such as improvised explosive devices (IEDs). These upgrades should allow the Leclerc to remain in service beyond 2040.[73] Starting in 2020, Nexter will begin delivering 200 "renovated Leclerc" tanks along with 18 "renovated DCL [*Dépanneur du Char Leclerc*]"—a type of armored recovery vehicle that specifically goes with the Leclerc tank. The combined effects of these upgrades will allow the Leclerc to operate better within GTIAs in the future.[74]

Collaborative Protection

Among the capabilities promised by the SCORPION program is what the French call *collaborative protection*, which they indicate the Leclerc and the VBCI are already capable of. The best description comes from an officer at the French Army's cavalry school in Saumur. According to him, the SCORPION vehicles will receive alerts from different on-board sensors (such as the Thales Antares) and analyze the data, sharing the results with "other actors concerned by the detected threat."[75] Then, depending on the computer system's analysis, the vehicle will either react automatically to protect the vehicle or propose a reaction that the crew can choose to validate or ignore. Automatic reactions might include nonlethal responses, such as setting off a smoke screen or jamming. The system is designed not to fire any lethal munitions automatically, but it has a *slew to cue* capability, meaning that the vehicle's gun might point automatically at the threat. However, the crew can decide how automatically it wants the system to run,

---

[69] Petit, 2018.

[70] Thales, "Savez-vous qui sont le VBMR et l'EBRC?" webpage, January 12, 2015.

[71] Michel Cabirol, "Défense: l'armée de Terre va enfin changer ses vieux 'chameaux,'" *La Tribune*, December 6, 2014.

[72] Petit, 2018.

[73] Nexter Group, "SCORPION Programme: LECLERC Tank Renovation Launched," press release, March 12, 2015.

[74] Ministère des Armées, "Programme Scorpion: lancement de la rénovation du char Leclerc," webpage, March 27, 2015.

[75] Email correspondence with a French Army officer at the Cavalry School in Saumur, France, July 12, 2018.

with the general guidance being to place it on automatic (except for firing munitions) during "offensive operations" but take the system off automatic for defensive operations. Ultimately, according to the French armor officer, the goal is to maximize the crew's chance of survival and "increase significantly the chances of rapidly neutralizing the threat."[76] This is called "collaborative" because it is not necessarily the most threatened crew that will take charge of neutralizing the threat, but instead "another actor well placed for it."[77]

Automation

One intriguing feature of collaborative warfare is the potential for full automation. The French Army's policy is not to automate the firing of lethal ammunition and instead to ensure that there is always a "man in the loop." The reasons commonly cited for this policy include the perceived heightened risk of causing collateral damage and fratricide, as well as the potential for savvy adversaries to trick automated weapons systems. Nonetheless, there is an understanding that full automation—with the implied reliance on artificial intelligence—offers the possibility of significantly speeding up the decision cycle and making one's forces far more responsive. One French senior officer, when asked about the possibility of setting SCORPION weapons systems on full automatic, did not answer the question but instead voiced the opinion that whether they desired it or not, fully automated firing is all but inevitable, especially in the closer quarters of urban warfare, where reaction times often are more limited than when fighting in open terrain.[78] He suggested that an adversary most likely would be the one to cross that line, at which point one's own forces would be obliged to follow suit.

Embarked Simulation

One of the more intriguing capabilities built into SCORPION technology is what the French call *simulation embarquée* (SEMBA), or embarked simulation, which is the ability to conduct simulation training inside actual vehicles wherever they happen to be. In embarked simulation, each vehicle becomes a simulator and the technology is both networked and scalable. One can put "two to three squadrons on simulators" and connect them, allowing them to fight together or against one another.[79] The simulators allow one to do "exercises and real maneuvers" and pair them with virtual roads, obstacles, and enemies. Some of the simulations take place while the vehicles are standing still with all the action entirely virtual, but the available sources indicate an augmented reality capability, meaning that they will conduct maneuvers in the real world and deal with virtual threats generated by the simulation software. The French Army sees clear

---

[76] Email correspondence with a French Army officer at the Cavalry School in Saumur, France, July 12, 2018.

[77] Email correspondence with a French Army officer at the Cavalry School in Saumur, France, July 12, 2018.

[78] Interview with a French Army general outside Paris, France, March 14, 2018.

[79] Interview with French Army officers at the Cavalry School in Saumur, France, March 12, 2018.

advantages in this capability, including the ability to log more training time because of units' ability to run simulations any time and any place.[80]

Differences Between SCORPION and FCS

The French, cognizant of the failure of the analogous American program (FCS), draw distinctions between SCORPION and FCS that make them more confident of SCORPION's success. Perhaps the most important distinction is a sense of SCORPION's relative modesty and the incremental way in which the French have gone about developing networked warfare technology. Another distinction is the sense that they are tailoring SCORPION to meet France's current doctrine and force structure, whereas FCS—and the U.S. effort to incorporate networked warfare beginning in the 1990s with programs like AAN and Strike Force—began with the technology and with the assumption that it would be correct to tailor doctrine and force structure around it.[81] One can argue that the U.S. Army aspired to force an RMA. In contrast, in the 1990s, the French had already undertaken a transformation in the literal sense when they decided to recast their ground forces along the lines of their expeditionary professional forces. They also undertook a transformation when they abandoned full divisions in favor of the modular GTIA and SGTIA—choices made entirely independent of technological considerations. To the French, NCW technology was meant to enhance what they were doing anyway, not precipitate major changes.[82] One might also argue, moreover, that the French, by aiming lower with respect to technological innovations, might have been more realistic about what they hoped to achieve, with the result that SCORPION is on schedule. Relatedly, the French also insist that, in contrast to the Americans, they do not regard technology as an end in itself. At most, they say, technology is a tool.

---

[80] Éléonore Krempff, "La révolution de l'armée de Terre en marche," *Armées d'aujourd'hui*, No. 390, June 2014, p. 40.

[81] Interview with Foundation for Strategic Research and Défense and Sécurité Internationale scholars in Paris, France, March 9, 2018.

[82] Interview with Foundation for Strategic Research and Défense and Sécurité Internationale scholars in Paris, France, March 9, 2018.

CHAPTER FOUR

The French Army's Operating Experience with Networked Warfare

Given the incremental nature of its development of NCW technologies, the French Army has made an effort to learn from its experience as it has operated with NCW in the field. From 2006 to the present, the French tested these technologies in series of small-scale (brigade size and below) expeditionary operations, mostly in semi-permissive environments in Africa.[1] In this chapter, we provide an overview of the French Army's operational experience, the lessons it learned, and the insights the experience has provided. By and large, the French give NEB 1.0 qualified approval. It has value, although not as much as one might have hoped. Their reasoning as to why the technology underperforms is of particular interest. In any case, the French are optimistic that SCORPION will have better results, largely because they are hopeful that it will address the shortcomings of NEB 1.0.

The 2006 Côte d'Ivoire *Retour d'Expérience*

As the French fielded NCW technology, they experimented with its use and documented lessons learned to benefit future development. Two important field tests took place in 2006. The first consisted of fielding a fully digitized brigade—the 6th Light Armored Brigade or *6e Brigade Légère Blindée*—to Côte d'Ivoire as part of Operation Unicorn. At roughly the same time, the French conducted an exercise using a second digitized brigade, the 2nd Armored Brigade or *2e Brigade Blindée*. The Côte d'Ivoire deployment is of particular interest because the French published a detailed lessons learned study (in French, *Retour d'Expérience*, or RETEX), which is the most complete RETEX on networked warfare that is openly available. According to the Côte d'Ivoire RETEX,

> The development of NEB permits the better sharing of information and preserving, through that information sharing, *subsidiarité*, which is the degree of initiative

---

[1]   The French Army also has simulated larger-scale, higher-end conflict.

of each echelon in the maneuver. The technology favors access to useful information, makes coordination easier thanks to the sharing of a common vision of the situation and guaranteeing a better reactivity and a greater complementarity.[2]

The study identifies other positives. One is that the technology "facilitates the internal re-articulation of a constituted unit," meaning how a unit organizes itself.[3] The study continues,

> The speed of the transmission of information permits one to exploit the detected vulnerabilities of an adversary, and to measure more closely the relationship of local forces and thus to seize, alongside the planned action, opportunities. These capacities contribute to responsiveness and, thus, the reversibility of a force, an advantage that is particularly appreciable for dealing rapidly with the versatility of a situation in the stabilization phase.[4]

This language echoes Hubin and the French emphasis on maneuver and *subsidiarité*. Indeed, elsewhere, the RETEX asserts that digitization in Côte d'Ivoire "permitted a greater decentralization of the actions of the GTIA, permitting a more dynamic and supple maneuver."[5] Another advantage was that the technology clearly enabled GTIAs to cover a larger geographic area than a nondigitized GTIA could, a fact that "seemed particularly advantageous for missions of zone control [wide area security] in the stabilization phase in a large theater."[6] The technology—in particular the improved navigation systems—also "accelerated the execution of indirect fires and improved their precision."[7] "By authorizing a supple and reactive fire maneuver," the study continued, the technology "modified the problem of concentration of efforts and permitted a better gradation of effects, which is really important in stabilization operations."[8] All of this comes with an important caveat: The RETEX recognizes that Côte d'Ivoire was a permissive environment, one in which the enemy did not deliberately attempt to blunt the advantages of the technology or even exploit it to its benefit, as was the case with Hezbollah in its 2006 war with Israel.[9]

The Côte d'Ivoire RETEX identifies various obstacles and limitations, including the following:

---

[2]   Centre de Doctrine d'Emploi des Forces, 2007, p. 9.

[3]   Centre de Doctrine d'Emploi des Forces, 2007, p. 9.

[4]   Centre de Doctrine d'Emploi des Forces, 2007, p. 9.

[5]   Centre de Doctrine d'Emploi des Forces, 2007, p. 21.

[6]   Centre de Doctrine d'Emploi des Forces, 2007, p. 21.

[7]   Centre de Doctrine d'Emploi des Forces, 2007, p. 21.

[8]   Centre de Doctrine d'Emploi des Forces, 2007, p. 21.

[9]   Centre de Doctrine d'Emploi des Forces, 2007, p. 17.

1. The efficacy of the technology depended heavily on the interoperability of different systems and even different versions of the same software.[10] Improving interoperability must be a priority.[11]
2. Digitized and nondigitized units can work together, but making that happen adds to the headquarters' work burden and slows it down, limiting the advantages of fielding the technology.[12]
3. To keep the technology from being a distraction, networked units have to deploy with robust information technology support.[13]
4. Managing the mass of data to ensure that each user has the right information at the right time remains a challenge; indeed, the system's ability to convert "information superiority" to a "true decisional superiority" is far from certain.[14]
5. The risk is real that commanders' greater and more detailed operational picture might tempt them to micromanage subordinates and undermine *subsidiarité*.[15]
6. There is a real danger of placing too much confidence in the technology and of viewing information as an end in itself. ("Information is only worth the operational use made of it.")[16]
7. Networked forces have to have "information management cells," the role of which consists of handling data (selecting, formatting, presenting, stocking, protecting, and destroying it) and distributing information about the handling of those data to units before the engagement.[17]
8. Although the technology favors the diffusion of orders through graphical means, the ability to transmit orders by voice has to be maintained in order to manage delicate situations in emergencies.[18]
9. The technology does not adequately model the organization and intentions of environmental factors that are so crucial in stabilization operations, such as mobs, armed groups, and nongovernmental organizations.[19]

---

[10] Centre de Doctrine d'Emploi des Forces, 2007, p. 17.

[11] Centre de Doctrine d'Emploi des Forces, 2007, p. 23.

[12] Centre de Doctrine d'Emploi des Forces, 2007, p. 18.

[13] Centre de Doctrine d'Emploi des Forces, 2007, p. 18.

[14] Centre de Doctrine d'Emploi des Forces, 2007, p. 18.

[15] Centre de Doctrine d'Emploi des Forces, 2007, pp. 18–19.

[16] Centre de Doctrine d'Emploi des Forces, 2007, p. 18.

[17] Centre de Doctrine d'Emploi des Forces, 2007, p. 19.

[18] Centre de Doctrine d'Emploi des Forces, 2007, p. 20.

[19] Centre de Doctrine d'Emploi des Forces, 2007, p. 20.

10. The technology absolutely has to become easier to use, more practical, and more compact—compactness is essential for facilitating its use at lower levels and in ad hoc command posts.[20]

11. Effective use of networked technology requires that its users at all levels have a high degree of technical proficiency, which requires a significant investment in training; there must be enough sufficiently qualified people on hand to permit 24-hour operations.[21]

12. High-bandwidth transmissions are a must.[22]

13. Digitization may lead to operators forgetting how to operate without it in degraded situations; traditional knowledge, such as working with paper maps, must be retained.[23]

Post-2006 Operational Experience

After Côte d'Ivoire, the French have deployed with at least some networked warfare technology in nearly every operation, including in Afghanistan, Mali, the Central African Republic, Lebanon, and in current operations in the Sahel and in Iraq and Syria. Comments by the officers interviewed for this study indicate that the value of the technology has been moderate at best. It might have helped, but it has not made a decisive difference and by no means has altered how the French Army organizes its forces and fights. Interestingly, the officers do not conclude that the concept of networked warfare and all of its ostensible promises are wrong and that they made a bad bet. Rather, they conclude that, to some extent, French Army officers are to blame for being too resistant to the technology's use, and the technology is to blame for being too difficult to use. The hope is that by improving the technology—SCORPION is intended to be a major step forward in that regard—and by cultivating within the Army a greater culture of networked warfare, the French Army's bet will at last begin to yield real dividends.

Afghanistan

French officers suggested that the technology provided some advantages in Afghanistan, but its potential was limited by two factors in addition to the aforementioned issue of French officers' frequent failure to use the technology as fully as they might have. One factor has to do with the nature of the conflict itself and with France's role within it. The other has to do with interoperability with U.S. forces.

---

[20] Centre de Doctrine d'Emploi des Forces, 2007, p. 22.

[21] Centre de Doctrine d'Emploi des Forces, 2007, pp. 24, 25.

[22] Centre de Doctrine d'Emploi des Forces, 2007, p. 24.

[23] Centre de Doctrine d'Emploi des Forces, 2007, p. 24.

Generally speaking, French Army commentary on Afghanistan reflects profound frustration with the war. One important source of frustration is the sense that the French Army conducted its portion of the war in a manner diametrically opposed to French conceptions of how to fight a war. There was little maneuver; rarely did French forces—or coalition forces, for that matter—take and hold the initiative. Instead, they ceded surprise to the enemy.[24] The French operated out of fixed positions, or forward operating bases (FOBs), from which they sortied patrols and conducted various other activities. "Nearly everyone knew whenever anyone left the FOB," writes Lieutenant Colonel Rémy Hémez, and coalition operations "followed a predictable pattern of preparation/action/disengagement."[25] One can also find expressions of resentment within the ranks over what some saw as France's willingness to defer to the U.S. strategy in Afghanistan and basically fight the United States' way.[26] However, seldom, if ever, has anyone within the French national security establishment, civilian or military, articulated clearly how France might have conducted the war if it had its druthers. In any case, from the French perspective, the Army is designed for fast-paced maneuver by relatively autonomous SGTIAs and GTIAs led by officers schooled in concepts such as the *effet majeur* and audacity. The technology, moreover, is intended to facilitate that way of warfighting. It follows, then, that if the Army were to fight significantly differently, the technology might prove less than useful.

The other issue is interoperability with U.S. forces. Although openly available French sources do not dwell at length on interoperability with respect to networked warfare with U.S. forces, it is fair to characterize the experience as both good and bad. The good is that French officers were able to link the nations' information systems using NATO information standards sufficiently well to permit the exchange of essential information, particularly with respect to unit locations (i.e., BFT), fires, and other forms of support.[27] The bad is that the exchange of information was not as free and full as desired in order to take advantage of the networked warfare capabilities of either side's systems. In fact, French officials indicated that the need for interoperability made it necessary for them to forgo some of the tools at their disposal.[28] One officer interviewed complained, for example, that while he was embedded in a U.S. headquarters, he was barred access to the U.S. Secret Internet Protocol Router (SIPR) network, forcing him to get critical information only by asking his American peers and getting their

---

[24] Hémez, 2016, p. 31.

[25] Hémez, 2016, p. 31.

[26] For a discussion of French criticism of the U.S. "way of war" in Afghanistan, see Michael Shurkin, "Meet France's War Philosophers," *War on the Rocks*, January 5, 2018. See also Nathalie Guibert, "'On ne peut pas faire la guerre contre le moral des soldats,'" *Le Monde*, July 1, 2010; and Desportes, 2015.

[27] Olivier Meriau, Anne-Henry Budan de Russé, and Rémi Pellabeuf, "Une approche pragmatique: la numérisation sur le théâtre afghan," *Doctrine Tactique*, No. 27, June 2013, p. 43.

[28] Meriau, Russé, and Pellabeuf, 2013, p. 42.

answers.[29] When they could link their systems, the exchange was suboptimal. According to an article on the subject in a French Army publication,

> The advance brought about by NEB in effect was constrained by the technological standards of our partners. . . . Developed to work according to our logic, NEB does not easily adapt to the constraints of the allies.

> Thus, the procedures . . . and materials used by [the International Security Assistance Force] are largely incompatible with ours. They can be made to work together but at the price of a loss of the efficacy brought by these technologies. Because the allies cannot directly exploit the digital outputs of SIR, it is not possible to directly integrate [concepts of operations] in the NEB.[30]

The French in Afghanistan after 2009 deployed at least the basic elements of NEB 1.0, including SICF; SIR; and HF, VHF, and satellite communications systems.[31] Some deployed with FELIN. According to one of the few openly available publications on the subject, the system was able to provide the brigade-level headquarters of Task Force Lafayette with precise real-time information about unit location (BFT, if the units had it) via the operational headquarters of the two GTIAs deployed in Kapisa and Surobi.[32] The technology also enabled them to keep a constant watch over the movements of the Task Force's route-clearing detachment, which was a special-purpose Mine-Resistant Ambush Protected (MRAP)–equipped engineering unit that cleared mines, as well as over the movements of logistical convoys that supplied the GTIAs.[33] Information about the convoys flowed through the headquarters of a logistical battalion.[34] There reportedly were some hiccups associated with the limitations of France's communications gear, especially PR4G, because of distances and the need for greater bandwidth. The Task Force coped by "doubling the network" and deploying VAB VENUS—a command variant of the VAB armored personnel carrier capable of satellite communications. These measures took care of the problems associated with distances and bandwidth.[35]

One of the stars of the French system deployed to Afghanistan reportedly was software hosted on SICF—an app, essentially—that greatly assisted in the analysis, collection, and dissemination of intelligence information for the benefit not only of the

---

[29] Interview with French Army colonel in Lille, France, June 19, 2015.

[30] Meriau, Russé, and Pellabeuf, 2013, p. 46.

[31] Meriau, Russé, and Pellabeuf, 2013, p. 42.

[32] Meriau, Russé, and Pellabeuf, 2013, p. 42.

[33] Meriau, Russé, and Pellabeuf, 2013, p. 42.

[34] Meriau, Russé, and Pellabeuf, 2013, p. 42.

[35] Meriau, Russé, and Pellabeuf, 2013, p. 46.

brigade-level intelligence section, but also for maneuver units.[36] Another star reportedly was FELIN. According to one source, "Even though there remains room for improvement, NEB with FELIN incontestably assures us a true technological superiority in the context of an asymmetrical conflict."[37] Precisely how and to what degree FELIN helped remains unclear. All in all, with regard to operations in Afghanistan, "the added value of NEB is undeniable" at the battalion level and below.[38]

African Operations: Central Africa and the Sahel

France's more recent military operations in Africa—Serval (the 2013 intervention in Mali), Sangaris (the 2013 intervention in the Central African Republic), and Barkhane (France's ongoing operations in the Sahel)—probably have benefited less from NEB than the Afghanistan operation. The conflicts are lower on the conflict spectrum and thus are arguably less amenable to the kinds of value added ostensibly provided by networked warfare technology. Moreover, commanders deploying to participate in these operations generally only take portions of the technology, especially FELIN, which all agree is too heavy and performs poorly in the extreme heat of the Sahel.

The technology nonetheless appears to have helped the French Army conduct decentralized and distributed operations using small maneuver units—SGTIAs and smaller—separated by large distances and supported by relatively scarce yet precise air and artillery fires. The dispersion of ground forces over large areas was particularly extreme in the Central African Republic, where the French operated SGTIAs as their main maneuver units and then took up the practice of splitting their SGTIAs into two relatively autonomous combined arms formations known as combined arms detachments.[39] Some things could not be divided, and the French had to ensure close coordination to prevent some soldiers from becoming isolated.[40] The French found the need constantly to move the GTIAs around, alter their composition and structures, and generally spread their component units dangerously thin over large areas.[41] Good communication systems were essential. It is not clear to what extent NEB facilitated Sangaris, but one can assume that it facilitated the coordination of small units, logistics, and support that French forces in the Central African Republic required. It partially mitigated the risks associated with how the French were operating. Essentially, the technology helped them do better what they were already doing.

---

[36] Meriau, Russé, and Pellabeuf, 2013, pp. 43–44.

[37] Meriau, Russé, and Pellabeuf, 2013, p. 46.

[38] Meriau, Russé, and Pellabeuf, 2013, p. 46.

[39] Rémi Hémez and Aline Leboeuf, *Retours sur Sangaris: Entre stabilisation et protection des civils*, Paris: Institut Français des Relations Internationales, 2016, p. 23.

[40] Hémez and Leboeuf, 2016, p. 23.

[41] Hémez and Leboeuf, 2016, p. 24.

NEB has, according to one source, benefited French forces in the Sahel by speeding up responsiveness to enemy actions at the lowest tactical levels. The action might only involve a few people or a single truck. Still, the digitization "helps to fuse information about the enemy," enabling them to respond quickly and share scant resources, resulting in a more capable force.[42]

One of the limitations of France's NEB that became apparent in both the Sahel and Afghanistan was the ability of French communication networks to handle large distances. VHF was inadequate, and the French Army does not have enough satellite communications capability at the platoon level, which was particularly relevant because of the small scale of French maneuver units in the region.[43] Therefore, the French adapted using HF with SIR and SITEL in command vehicles and using HF to relay satellite communications. This solution had been discovered in Afghanistan. According to one interviewee, soldiers were able to double the satellite capability available for use at the company level using HF. "This is important," he said, "because we don't have any money."[44] He added that it enabled the French to have units operating 1,000 km from their commanders.[45]

In practice, the French tend to deploy only with some parts of the technology, and in fact they cite the ability to treat the technology as modular as a virtue. The French also want modularity to be a design feature in future iterations of the technology. They acknowledge, however, that they might have gotten more out of the technology had they brought more of it with them and used it, but generally officers tend not to see its utility or think it is too difficult to use. In the case of desert operations, some officers see the technology as inappropriate for the climate. There is also a generational difference at play: Older officers are less interested in or comfortable with the technology, whereas younger officers are more likely to regard it as a normal part of doing business.

Indeed, a striking feature of nearly all of the French Army commentary on its experience with this technology is the importance of developing a culture of networked warfare. Using the technology has to come naturally and with the expectation that expert use would enable users to fully exploit the technology. Only then would the Army finally would get the full value from it. In other words, the French concede that the technology has not fulfilled its promise, and they believe that part of the problem is that they simply have not been using it as much as or as effectively as they could have been. One reason for this lack of use is that the technology arguably is of limited use for many of the operations French soldiers conduct and the French tend to leave parts of it behind when they deploy. Of course, the soldiers might be underestimating its value, owing to their limited understanding of what it can do or how to use it. Their

---

[42] Interview with French Army officers at STAT in Versailles, France, March 6, 2018.

[43] Interview with French Army officers at STAT in Versailles, France, March 6, 2018.

[44] Interview with French Army officers at STAT in Versailles, France, March 6, 2018.

[45] Interview with French Army officers at STAT in Versailles, France, March 6, 2018.

conservatism plays a part, although so, too, does the admitted difficulty of using the technology. It can be cumbersome and time-consuming. All commentators give their technology poor grades for ergonomics, so improved ergonomics are essential. Many also are optimistic that the rising generation of French officers, having been exposed to the technology for their entire careers, are naturally more comfortable with it.

Does Network-Centric Warfare Technology Make a Difference?

In light of the various reservations expressed earlier, the question of the value of NCW technology, whether NEB 1.0 or SCORPION, remains to be answered. When asked directly, French officers and other experts give it guarded approval. Basically, the technology helps, but it does not represent an RMA.

For example, when interviewed for this study, French Army officers at France's cavalry school in Saumur gave NEB 1.0 generally positive grades.[46] It has not fundamentally changed how the French fight, they said, but it has brought the following concrete advantages:

- better comprehension of the situation horizontally and vertically
- more-rapid transmission and completion of orders
- faster decisionmaking
- better coordination of units
- better optimization of resources
- more-precise effects
- more-effective SGTIAs.

French officers acknowledged that the impact of NEB technology on lower-end operations has been minimal. For example, they asserted that it made little difference for Operation Serval in Mali or Operation Sangaris in the Central African Republic.[47] For higher-intensity operations—tank warfare, for example—they saw the technology as an enhancement but not a game-changer. Moreover, NEB technology does not enable the Army to do more with fewer tanks. According to one officer, "A balance of power remains the balance of power," and five networked Leclercs cannot replace ten.[48] The technology is no substitute for mass in situations in which mass counts.

In an interview for this research, a networked warfare expert at the French Army's Ground Forces Command in Lille broke down the advantages of NEB 1.0 by echelon.

---

[46] Interview with French Army officers at the Cavalry School in Saumur, France, March 12, 2018.

[47] Interview with French Army officers at the Cavalry School in Saumur, France, March 12, 2018.

[48] Interview with French Army officers at the Cavalry School in Saumur, France, March 12, 2018. Given that the French Army, like its other Western counterparts, has not fought a conventional armor battle in decades, this calculation is theoretical.

At the divisional and brigade levels, he said, the technology does in fact speed up the decision cycle. "It works," he said, and noted further than the experience was very positive.[49] He also noted as a benefit a quieter headquarters in which greater collaboration takes place. This is partly because everyone in a command post has the same operational picture. There is a greater flow of information and a lot more information. The catch, however, is that access to so much information increases the risk of commanders involving themselves in matters they should be leaving to their subordinates. He also was concerned that commanders might be under the impression that they know everything, and he said that working with units that are less digitized slows everything down. From the battalion level down, results are less clear because of several factors, including poor integration of the many systems of lower-echelon operations. The officer was optimistic, however, that the improvements that SCORPION is expected to bring will make an important difference, although he did note that he was not expecting anything revolutionary. SCORPION, he said, would be no more than an incremental improvement. Significant, but incremental.[50]

Impact on French Army Doctrine

France's networked warfare technology as it exists today has not prompted the Army to redesign the force structure, alter its doctrine in any significant way, or change how it fights wars. In general, the French downplay the technology's impact, describing it in terms of enhancing and enabling what they do but not precipitating fundamental changes. If anything, according to one officer, the French experience has taught them not to be ambitious. Furthermore, they believe that the aspect of the technology that has made the most difference—the one really revolutionary part—is BFT.[51] When asked how a company-sized task force (SGTIA) in 2018 compared with a predigital 1998 SGTIA, one officer responded that the contemporary force, primarily because of BFT, was more "fluid," could be more ambitious (because one knew where one's forces were located), and could plan and react more quickly because of nearly instant access to information regarding unit location.[52] Messaging was also cited as a real gain.[53] Several officers and civilian experts interviewed for this study argued that NEB 1.0 is underused, adding to the aforementioned constraints the fact that not all vehicles are

---

[49] Interview with French Army officer at Commandement des Forces Terrestres in Lille, France, March 14, 2018.

[50] Interview with French Army officer at Commandement des Forces Terrestres in Lille, France, March 14, 2018.

[51] Interview with French Army officers at French Army General Staff in Paris, France, March 9, 2018.

[52] Interview with French Army officers at French Army General Staff in Paris, France, March 9, 2018.

[53] Interview with Foundation for Strategic Research and Défense et Sécurité Internationale scholars in Paris, France, March 9, 2018.

equipped with it, and in units with mixed levels of technology, the whole defaults to the lowest common denominators.[54]

This does not mean that the French do not intend to change their force structure or doctrine in light of their experience with SCORPION. In fact, the French Army—and, in particular, the SCORPION Battle Lab run by CDEC, the French equivalent of TRADOC, along with other groups in France's various schools—are running simulations and conducting experiments for that purpose. There is, for example, a test-bed SCORPION unit known as the SCORPION Combat Expert Force, or *Force d'expertise du combat SCORPION* that conducts experiments.[55] The Battle Lab published an exploratory first draft of SCORPION doctrine in 2014 and another draft in 2017.[56] Both drafts are classified. According to the director of the SCORPION Battle Lab, the drafts' focus has been on "big ideas," with a considerable distance remaining between them and practical application.[57]

Interestingly, the Battle Lab director said that earlier futuristic writings such as Hubin's are no longer seen as far-fetched, and the Battle Lab has been experimenting with organizational structures that break with extant French doctrine.[58] He said that among the developments they have been testing are pushing additional capabilities to the GTIA and generally flattening the GTIA command structure.[59] The capabilities they are pushing down to the GTIA include intelligence and what he described as "discovery and investigative capabilities," which are roughly equivalent to reconnaissance functions.[60]

What French Networked Warfare Technology Is Good For

One of the unanswered questions about French military modernization is "modernization for what," or what precisely do these new capabilities allow the French Army to do now or do better than before. In interviews, the answer was less than clear. Perhaps because French military modernization must fit inside a tight defense budget, the party line was that "SCORPION is for all types of conflict—communications system adapted to different types of conflict, irrespective of level of intensity."[61] On

---

[54] Interview with Foundation for Strategic Research and Défense and Sécurité Internationale scholars in Paris, France, March 9, 2018.

[55] Interview with SCORPION Battle Lab director in Paris, France, March 8, 2018.

[56] Interview with SCORPION Battle Lab director in Paris, France, March 8, 2018.

[57] Interview with SCORPION Battle Lab director in Paris, France, March 8, 2018.

[58] Interview with SCORPION Battle Lab director in Paris, France, March 8, 2018.

[59] Interview with SCORPION Battle Lab director in Paris, France, March 8, 2018.

[60] Interview with SCORPION Battle Lab director in Paris, France, March 8, 2018.

[61] Interview with French Army officer at the École de Transmissions in Cesson-Sévigné, France, March 13, 2018.

closer examination, it remains an open question whether SCORPION is, indeed, a full-spectrum capability as advertised.

Many French officers argued that while the equipment could be used anywhere, the benefits of NCW technology would mostly be felt at the higher end of conflict. There was a general belief that NCW capabilities are overkill for low-intensity combat in Africa. As one French officer remarked, "Serval—any GTIA can do this—so there is a recognition that [the] Army needs to think less about Serval and more about Ukraine."[62] The SCORPION Battle Lab therefore was not modeling Serval-type operations. Although the lab does not explicitly conduct simulations using Ukraine or Syria as models, it does simulate operating against enemies that have the kinds of capabilities one finds in those theaters, one of which is air superiority.[63] Another capability is the advantage that they saw networked warfare technology giving adversaries in Ukraine and Syria, especially links between observers and fires. "We watched the advantage that digitization gave the Russians in Ukraine . . . and we saw something similar in Syria," where the "Russians improved the capabilities of the Syrians."[64] This improved above all the effectiveness of artillery and made it "once again" the "centerpiece of the battlefield," which has important implications for offensive and defensive operations, particularly against an opponent that might simply have a greater ability to mass fires.[65] As one officer put it, "dispersion and decentralization were always taken into account. SCORPION was always built for high-intensity" conflict.[66] Similarly, another officer claimed, "NEB is, above all, for high-technology war. You will see the most advantages from NEB in high-intensity wars."[67]

By contrast, outside interlocutors were generally more skeptical of NCW technology's utility in high-intensity conflict, arguing that the Army is overselling the technology's true value added, and SCORPION remains at the "mid-to-low end of the spectrum."[68] As one defense analyst remarked, the "Army probably really does mean [that SCORPION is designed for] full-spectrum [operations], but that might not be true in reality. In a closed-door parliamentary session, the Army representative dis-

---

[62] Second interview with French Army officers at Centre de Doctrine et d'Enseignement du Commandement in Paris, France, March 8, 2018.

[63] Interview with SCORPION Battle Lab director in Paris, France, March 8, 2018.

[64] Interview with French Army officers at Centre de Doctrine et d'Enseignement du Commandement in Paris, France, March 7, 2018.

[65] Interview with SCORPION Battle Lab director in Paris, France, March 8, 2018; Interview with French Army officers at Centre de Doctrine et d'Enseignement du Commandement in Paris, France, March 7, 2018.

[66] Interview with French Army officers at Centre de Doctrine et d'Enseignement du Commandement in Paris, France, March 7, 2018.

[67] Interview with French Army officers at the Cavalry School in Saumur, France, March 12, 2018.

[68] Interview with Foundation for Strategic Research and Défense et Sécurité Internationale scholars in Paris, France, March 9, 2018.

cussed advantages of SCORPION but did not take into account scenarios where they might be fighting against an enemy like Russia in Ukraine (with high-end electronic warfare)."[69]

Indeed, when pressed, interviewees noted that many of the details of how SCORPION would fare in a high-intensity combat seemed vague. Although most officers argued that SCORPION was designed with electronic warfare in mind, few believed that the capability had been thoroughly tested against a realistic depiction of what Russia could deploy or that the Army had adequately prioritized this area.[70] Without taking an adversary's electronic warfare capabilities into consideration, the French Army reportedly is still struggling to deconflict its CONTACT radio system with its barrage jammers and maintain interoperability standards.[71] Even questions about how a medium-weight force will be able to destroy heavy Russia forces remain open to debate. A minority of French officers stated directly that they do not foresee a scenario in which France would ever fight Russian troops.[72]

Perhaps the most honest assessment of SCORPION's capabilities came from one French officer, who argued that it was a medium-weight solution to medium-type problems. He noted that "you have a theater that is stable on one end; on the other end, you have an unstable, non-permissive theater. NEB is made for both these kinds of theater but gives you the most added-value for conflicts that are in the medium state between these two extremes."[73] In practice, this means a more intense environment than in many of the Africa missions, but a less intense environment than envisioned in a war in the Baltics—an environment more similar to those faced in Afghanistan or in the 2006 Lebanon War. Ultimately, how SCORPION will perform in any of these environments remains an unanswered question.

That said, French officials approach the prospect of high-intensity conflict from a particular perspective. One aspect of this perspective is the extremely low probability that France will find itself having to conduct such a war on its own. One officer asserted that "we know that if we fight Russia we won't be alone."[74] The French assume that they need to think about high-intensity warfare in a coalition context. This arguably comforts them in their choice to focus on the "median segment" of the conflict

---

[69] Discussion with IFRI scholars in Paris, France, March 7, 2018.

[70] Interview with Foundation for Strategic Research and Défense and Sécurité Internationale scholars in Paris, France, March 9, 2018.

[71] Interview with French Army officers at French Army General Staff in Paris, France, March 9, 2018.

[72] Second interview with French Army officers at Centre de Doctrine et d'Enseignement du Commandement in Paris, France, March 8, 2018.

[73] Interview with French Army officer at Commandement des Forces Terrestres in Lille, France, March 14, 2018.

[74] Interview with French Army officers at Centre de Doctrine et d'Enseignement du Commandement in Paris, France, March 7, 2018.

spectrum, which they see as the most realistic given France's resources.[75] As one officer explained, "we're sticking to the median solution because it's the best we can afford."[76]

Other officers voiced skepticism about the French Army's preparedness for high-intensity warfare, noting that armies tend to "be what they do." Similarly, the way French officers talk about conflicts that they sometimes describe as high-intensity—Afghanistan among them (not the conflict as a whole but particular battles)—suggests that their definition of what constitutes "high-intensity" is different from U.S. definitions. One officer argued that the technology is of limited value at the two extreme ends of the conflict spectrum: At the highest intensity, commanders are too busy fighting to benefit from all the information provided to them, while low-intensity operations require access to information that the system is not designed to provide.[77] For example, low-intensity operations require high degrees of interagency coordination and access to open-source information. French networked warfare technology, he said, does nothing for interagency operations and does not interact with civilian networks, such as the internet.[78] In other words, the technology makes the most sense for the "middle" segment of the conflict spectrum. Lastly, the French acknowledge that the technology only partially makes up for ingredients that they regard as critical for prevailing in a high-intensity war (specifically, volume and massed fires).[79] This is, for them, one of the major lessons of the conflict in Ukraine.[80]

The question, then, is not so much the value of networked warfare technology but rather the capacity of the French Army to fight a high-intensity war, especially given its size. As one officer insisted, "to some extent [the technology] does make up for size . . . but we don't have any illusions about our mass." "We don't think," he continued, "that with more technology we could do a lot more things than we can now."[81] Similarly, French officers argued that the extent to which the technology makes up for quantity depends on the type of operation. In addition to its inability to compensate for massed fires, the technology cannot replace numbers when one needs to hold ter-

---

[75] Interview with French Army officers at Centre de Doctrine et d'Enseignement du Commandement in Paris, France, March 7, 2018.

[76] Interview with French Army officers at Centre de Doctrine et d'Enseignement du Commandement in Paris, France, March 7, 2018.

[77] Interview with French Army officer at Commandement des Forces Terrestres in Lille, France, March 14, 2018.

[78] Interview with French Army officer at Commandement des Forces Terrestres in Lille, France, March 14, 2018.

[79] Corentin Brustlein, *Maîtriser la puissance de feu: Un défi pour les forces terrestres*, Paris: IFRI, 2015, pp. 47–48.

[80] Interview with French Army officers at Centre de Doctrine et d'Enseignement du Commandement in Paris, France, March 7, 2018.

[81] Interview with French Army officers at Centre de Doctrine et d'Enseignement du Commandement in Paris, France, March 7, 2018.

ritory.[82] Instead, although most French officers welcomed improvements in communications and information-sharing, particularly for urban combat, they saw these differences as mattering only on the margins.[83] In keeping with the overall conception of SCORPION as an evolutionary rather than a revolutionary improvement, one French officer summed up the general attitude: "If numerical difference is not too great, then technology can make up the gap. Technology is good, but it's still a question of quantity. We have no illusions within the Army—we do not believe that we will be able to do a lot more stuff with the technology."[84]

There is also the question of whether the technology is suited for larger-scale operations than the kind in which the French Army has typically engaged. The last time the French deployed a full division was in 1991, when France participated in the U.S.-led coalition against Iraq. Since then, the French have not deployed more than a brigade-sized force, and most French combat deployments have been considerably smaller. In this case, the French acknowledge that they have not tested their networked warfare technology on brigade-and-above formations, and the GTIA remains front and center in their thinking about networked warfare operations, as well as in their testing and modeling.

Although France has found the technology helpful for covering larger geographic regions with relatively small deployments, it did not build its systems with vast operational spaces such as the Sahel in mind. On the contrary, France designed the system for the relatively smaller spaces of potential European battlefields. French officers noted that, in the Sahel, they were forced to place relatively scarce satellite communications capabilities in lower echelons than planned to link dispersed units because of expense.[85] They argued that their systems work better in peacekeeping operations in Lebanon because of their units' greater proximity to one another.[86]

One concern they have regarding SCORPION's appropriateness for high-intensity warfare is the amount of time required to set up a SCORPION command post. The French believe that they need to revive the Cold War doctrine of moving command posts often to prevent detection and targeting by the enemy. The rule is moving every ten hours for brigade headquarters, every 24 hours for division headquarters, and

---

[82] Interview with French Army officers at Centre de Doctrine et d'Enseignement du Commandement in Paris, France, March 7, 2018.

[83] Interview with French Army officers at the Cavalry School in Saumur, France, March 12, 2018.

[84] Second interview with French Army officers at Centre de Doctrine et d'Enseignement du Commandement in Paris, France, March 8, 2018.

[85] Interview with French Army officers at STAT in Versailles, France, March 6, 2018.

[86] Interview with French Army officers at STAT in Versailles, France, March 6, 2018. As of November 30, 2018, France had 668 service members in Lebanon as part of the United Nations Interim Force in Lebanon, making it one of the largest European contributors. See United Nations Interim Force in Lebanon, "UNIFIL Troop-Contributing Countries," webpage, November 30, 2018.

every 72 hours for the corps level.[87] Presently, and with the SCORPION systems now or soon to be coming online, the ten-hour requirement cannot be met.[88]

In any case, French officers insist that, increasingly, Western militaries are losing their technological edge as technology democratizes. As the SCORPION Battle Lab director put it, Syria proves that the West's technical superiority is over, because anyone can have an armed drone, for example.[89] Even networked warfare technology can be home-brewed using technology bought cheaply off the shelf.[90] The effort to maintain an edge is necessary, but future investments will bring diminishing returns. This means, officers insist, that armies will have to fall back on three things to prevail. The first is a qualitative edge having to do with the men and women commanding ground forces and using the technology. The second is their enduring *rusticité*, which comes into play in any degraded environment or when the two sides of a conflict are evenly matched in terms of technology. The third factor is numbers, the lack of which worries French officers and defense experts greatly.[91]

Network-Centric Warfare with Allies Is Still an Open Question

One of the more peculiar findings from our interviews is that the French Army does not seem to have a clear conception of how SCORPION will integrate into coalition operations. Coalition operations are inherently challenging for any version of networked warfare. There will almost invariably be technical and policy challenges to sharing information seamlessly across different nationalities. The challenge of implementing NCW, however, is particularly acute in the French context given the centrality of the assumption that French forces will "never fight alone" and the breadth of the type of partners French forces engage with on a regular basis.

On one end of the spectrum, French Army units routinely partner with relatively underdeveloped forces in Africa which will not be equipped with SCORPION technology. In general, French officers acknowledged the challenges of integrating these technologically unsophisticated allied forces in SCORPION formations.[92] Nonetheless, many felt that because the adversary was similarly nondigitized, the obstacles

---

[87] Personal communication with Elie Tenenbaum, November 22, 2018.

[88] Interview with French Army officer at the École de Transmissions in Cesson-Sévigné, France, March 13, 2018.

[89] Interview with SCORPION Battle Lab director in Paris, France, March 8, 2018.

[90] Interview with SCORPION Battle Lab director in Paris, France, March 8, 2018.

[91] Interview with French Army officer at Commandement des Forces Terrestres in Lille, France, March 14, 2018. One example of French Army concern over its size is a 2016 study by Rémy Hémez and Aline Leboeuf of the French intervention in the Central African Republic in 2013 (Hémez and Leboeuf, 2016). The study expresses acute concern over the gap between the size of the force doctrine suggested was necessary in the Central African Republic and the size of the force actually sent, and it examines some of the ramifications of the shortfall.

[92] Interview with French Army officers at French Army General Staff in Paris, France, March 9, 2018.

would not be insurmountable and, in most cases, radio communications between French and African forces would suffice.[93] Moreover, with SCORPION, French commanders could at least communicate and coordinate internally among all the various French elements on the battlefield.[94]

Perhaps a more vexing challenge becomes integrating fellow first-world militaries—including fellow NATO countries—for a high-intensity fight. Even in cases in which France has a habitual relationship with other NATO countries, it is still struggling to fully implement cross-national NCW. As of this writing, the Franco-German brigade operates using German combat information systems at the brigade and regimental level, which requires training French officers on it, embedding German liaison officers, and building some *passarelles* to enable information to flow between French and German systems.[95] According to a French officer with experience in the brigade, the arrangement requires addressing numerous doctrinal, policy, and technical issues related to classification and planning procedures. The arrangements work, but not without a lot of effort, and not without officers from both sides having to develop deep familiarity with how the two armies operate.[96] The French intend to bring SCORPION to the Franco-German brigade; it is not clear whether this will oblige the unit to migrate away from the German systems it currently uses.[97]

Similarly, an officer with experience building interoperability with the British for the sake of the Franco-British Combined Joint Expeditionary Force (CJEF) cited the need for similar levels of effort.[98] In the case of the CJEF, whichever country has the lead for a particular operation provides the information systems (the authors witnessed British officers using French systems at a CJEF command exercise held outside Paris in June 2015). A prominent problem the CJEF has encountered is related to the MR/MS split on the French side and the fact that British systems tend to be Secret at all levels. In practice, this means that at high command levels, where the French are using SICF and the British are using their MAGPIE information system, which are both Secret, there are fewer hurdles, but at lower echelons where the French use SIR (which is MR) and the British use BCIP (which is Secret), there are more problems. Many of the problems have been worked out through hard work and exercises, but it is noteworthy that the officer dismissed focusing on building technical solutions. He noted that technical solutions require a lot of time and expense, and the solutions developed tend to have

---

[93] Interview with French Army officer at the École de Transmissions in Cesson-Sévigné, France, March 13, 2018.

[94] Interview with French Army officer at the École de Transmissions in Cesson-Sévigné, France, March 13, 2018.

[95] Interview with French Army colonel in Lille, France, June 19, 2015.

[96] Interview with French Army colonel in Lille, France, June 19, 2015.

[97] Interview with French Army officers at French Army General Staff in Paris, France, March 9, 2018.

[98] Interview with French Army colonel in Lille, France, June 19, 2015.

a short shelf life because they may stop working when either force updates its technology. Rather than work toward seamlessly integrating information systems, the officer stressed, the better investment to make is in cultivating mutual familiarity.[99]

Ultimately, the French Army is still working through these technical and policy challenges, and French officers fall back on the conviction that where there is a will, there is a way, meaning that one way or another, they and their partners will find ways to overcome all of the many hurdles in the way of NCW in a coalition context. In the meantime, coalition operations probably will diminish the potential of the technology.

Network-Centric Warfare Can Provide Only Partial Situational Awareness

To date, the French experience only partially validates one of the central promises of NCW (specifically, that it improves situational awareness). Multiple French officers highlighted that one of the primary benefits of NEB has been better situational awareness on friendly or Blue Forces. As one senior French officer asserted, the "[f]og of war has been lifted regarding blue forces."[100] In particular, this French officer cited BFT with reducing the number of friendly fire incidents and speeding up the call for fire operations, particularly in joint American-French operations during the counter–Islamic State campaign in Iraq.[101]

At the same time, NCW at best can only provide situational awareness because it cannot detail where enemy or Red Forces are in real time. As one mid-grade French officer noted, "Troops [are] always complaining that they do not have enough information on the enemy."[102] Part of the lack of viable Red Force Tracking may be because of the type of irregular wars that France has confronted in Afghanistan, Iraq, and Africa; specifically, against enemies whose strategy hinged on their ability to blend into the population. Should France ever confront a more conventional threat, a Red Force Tracker may become more plausible. Still, at least some French officers believed that the lack of viable real-time Red Force Tracking is inherent in the nature of war, where surprise is a virtue and concealment is fundamental to maneuver. As one French officer noted, "There will never be a red force tracker, but the blue force tracker will be hugely important ([it is] already very important to know who your friends are—enormously reduces the fog of war)."[103]

Interestingly, many French officers were not only accepting of the reality of incomplete intelligence but suggested that in some respects it may be a virtue. Too

---

[99] Interview with French Army colonel in Lille, France, June 19, 2015.

[100] Interview with a senior French Army officer, Paris, France, March 9, 2018.

[101] Interview with French Army officers at STAT in Versailles, France, March 6, 2018; Interview with French Army officer at the École de Transmissions in Cesson-Sévigné, France, March 13, 2018.

[102] Interview with French Army officers at STAT in Versailles, France, March 6, 2018.

[103] Second interview with French Army officers at Centre de Doctrine et d'Enseignement du Commandement in Paris, France, March 8, 2018.

much intelligence, the argument went, inspired overconfidence and, ultimately, reck-lessness. One French officer remarked, "There is a danger to knowing everything or thinking that you know everything. The image could refresh constantly, but perhaps that's not such a good idea. If it doesn't refresh constantly, there remains some doubt in your mind, encouraging you to be more cautious."[104] Instead, soldiers should only have access to the intelligence "immediately relevant," knowing full well that they are acting on a partial picture of the full situation.[105]

All About Ergonomics?

Of course, how much intelligence soldiers receive on the tactical level is only partially a question of information collection and sharing; much of it comes down to how acces-sible that information is to the individual user. This, perhaps, is one of the central findings of the French experience with NCW technologies. Ergonomics—and the ease with which that technology can be used—plays a vital role in whether soldiers actu-ally use the technology once it is adopted and ultimately helps determine the success or failure of the overall system.

Getting the ergonomics right proves a particularly vexing challenge for rapidly evolving fields like military information technology. Given the challenges of develop-ing, testing, and fielding military technology that can operate in various conditions against different opponents, military technology also will inevitably fall behind its civilian counterparts. French officers by and large acknowledge this limitation, but have still tried to make the French military information technology as user-friendly as possible. As one officer remarked, "We cannot reach the same level of current smart-phone technologies, but we are working with adaptive processes."[106]

The French Army, however, has encountered ergonomic challenges with its mod-ernization program even outside the information technology realm. One of the central complaints about the new FELIN system is that it is too heavy, weighing as much as 40 kilos (or almost 90 pounds) per soldier.[107] Although the information technology embedded in FELIN allows platoon leaders to have better situational awareness on the tactical level and allows for soldiers to disperse over greater distances, sheer weight becomes a drag on the units' overall mobility.[108] (The French are developing FELIN 2.0, which is scheduled for fielding in 2021. It will presumably be lighter.)

---

[104] Interview with French Army officer at Commandement des Forces Terrestres in Lille, France, March 14, 2018.

[105] Interview with French Army officer at Commandement des Forces Terrestres in Lille, France, March 14, 2018.

[106] Interview with French Army officers at French Army General Staff in Paris, France, March 9, 2018.

[107] Interview with French Army officers at French Army General Staff in Paris, France, March 9, 2018.

[108] Interview with French Army officers at French Army General Staff in Paris, France, March 9, 2018.

In order to identify and correct these ergonomic problems, the French Army has an organization—STAT—that is responsible for field-testing new equipment.[109] STAT is staffed with Army officers and one of its key functions is collecting data about what soldiers like and do not like about new technology and then injecting this feedback back into the development process. Despite this process, the French Army continues to wrestle with these ergonomic obstacles to modernization.

Adoption of New Technology Has Cultural Second-Order Effects

The final lesson learned from the French experience is perhaps the most important, but also is the most amorphous of all—the interplay between culture and technology. Although much of the discussion about SCORPION and French NCW centers on its military utility, interviews with French officers suggested that military culture can have almost as much effect on whether and how a particular innovation gets employed. In France's case, the move to NCW ran headlong into two prevailing norms with in the French Army—*rusticité* and *subsidiarité*, or mission command.

Perhaps the less problematic of these two norms is *rusticité*. As a French defense analyst remarked, "Even today, there are commanders who are fully equipped with networked technology but who still go into battle with just half of equipment and consider it a virtue to be able to work with less."[110] Especially given that the "light" colonial forces (as opposed to the heavy armored European-based force) became dominant in the French Army during the post–Cold War drawdowns, the norm of *rusticité* led some French officers to shy away from embracing technology.[111]

As it turns out, so far, *rusticité* seems to offer an important advantage, which is that it means the French are serious about retaining the skills required to fight without the technology. Some expressed their belief that in conflicts with peer competitors who can negate the advantage provided by NCW technology, or who can shut down one's network through electronic warfare, the advantage then goes to the side that is most capable of operating without technology and in harsh conditions. The French think that aspect gives them an edge.

A potentially more significant cultural challenge of NCW is that of *subsidiarité* or mission command. Dating in part to its colonial roots, during which relatively small units would be operating independently and dispersed over a geographically large area, the French Army traditionally has had a principle of delegating authority to lower echelons—with each echelon getting general guidance from its higher headquarters but given relative freedom in terms of how to accomplish the mission at hand. As one French officer remarked, "For us, the principle of subsidiarity is completely inviolable.

---

[109] Interview with French Army officers at French Army General Staff in Paris, France, March 9, 2018; Interview with French Army officers at STAT in Versailles, France, March 6, 2018.

[110] Interview with IFRI scholars in Paris, France, March 7, 2018.

[111] Interview with IFRI scholars in Paris, France, March 7, 2018.

The commander, the lieutenant, the captain, etc. wins the war at his own level."[112] Improvements in information technology have the potential to challenge this norm. As the upper echelon commanders' ability to monitor developments at the tactical level from afar improves, there is newfound ability to centralize authorities at the senior levels.

Although most acknowledged the possibility of micromanagement because of improved NCW, French military officers were divided about whether these fears would come to pass. Some argued that the demands on senior leaders' time would prevent *entrisme* (micromanagement) and force them to delegate authority to lower echelons, especially in high-intensity warfare.[113] Others believed that the French Army's inherent culture bias toward an "eyes on, hands off" approach to command would shield against any tendency toward micromanagement.[114] Still, others were more dubious.

Ultimately, the discussion of SCORPION and NCW's impact on the norms *rusticité* and *subsidiarité* makes a larger point: Technology has important second-order effects that need to be considered in any plan for how to adopt new technologies. Developing new technology cannot simply be siloed within the technical aspects of the force but should consider how the end users approach and employ technology.[115] If not, cultural obstacles can impede progress almost as significantly as practical obstacles can. As one French officer remarked about the Army's slow adoption of networked warfare, "At the beginning, there were some people who were not prepared to accept it—it was too much; but [NCW] has gradually become implanted in their minds."[116]

---

[112] Interview with French Army officer at Commandement des Forces Terrestres in Lille, France, March 14, 2018.

[113] Interview with French Army officers at French Army General Staff in Paris, France, March 9, 2018; Interview with French Army officers at the Cavalry School in Saumur, France, March 12, 2018.

[114] Interview with French Army officers at STAT in Versailles, France, March 6, 2018; Second interview with French Army officers at Centre de Doctrine et d'Enseignement du Commandement in Paris, France, March 8, 2018.

[115] Second interview with French Army officers at Centre de Doctrine et d'Enseignement du Commandement in Paris, France, March 8, 2018.

[116] Interview with French Army officer at Commandement des Forces Terrestres in Lille, France, March 14, 2018.

CHAPTER FIVE

Conclusion: Implications for the U.S. Army

The French Army's experience with NCW technology and its qualified support for its benefits do not give the U.S. Army cause to rethink dramatically its procurement priorities, doctrine, or approach to the concept more broadly. If anything, the French experience likely reaffirms, although may not decisively prove (given that the French have yet to fully test NEB 2.0 in high-end combat) the U.S. Army's current skepticism about the central tenet of the 1990s version of RMA: *Better intelligence and communications does not compensate for mass, firepower, and protection.* Indeed, French interlocutors were very clear that even under the best circumstances, the intelligence picture is only partial (and is focused on friendly rather than enemy forces) and no amount of NEB compensates for adequate fire support or numbers.

Moreover, although more-detailed field-testing and engineering analysis would have to be done to reach a more definitive conclusion about how French networked warfare technology stacks up relative to comparable U.S. systems, the interviews with French Army officers seem to suggest that the equipment is mostly a French solution to a French problem stemming from French budgetary constraints—specifically, the need to build one middle-weight force that is deployable to Africa but that is still robust enough for higher-end threats. By contrast, the U.S. Army's current modernization challenge starts with a different strategic premise. The 2018 *National Defense Strategy* argues that "interstate strategic competition, not terrorism, is now the primary concern in U.S. national security."[1] Unlike the French modernization effort, which tries to build one force for all scenarios, the *National Defense Strategy* prioritizes the high-end fight against Russia and China in particular, assuming that the other adversaries are either lesser-included cases or areas where the United States must take risk.[2] Setting aside the wisdom of either the French or U.S. assumptions for a moment, the fact that the two countries have different starting points means that the U.S. Army has cause to make different trade-offs than the French Army does in terms of equipment and communications gear.

---

[1] DoD, *Summary of the 2018 National Defense Strategy: Sharpening the American Military's Competitive Edge,* Washington, D.C., January 2018, p. 1.

[2] DoD, 2018, p. 4.

Finally, there are few doctrinal lessons for the U.S. Army to learn from the French example. As mentioned, the French Army has not fully tested SCORPION at the brigade level, limiting the applicability of the example for the U.S. Army, which has built much of its force structure around the brigade. Even at the lower level, SCORPION seems to be refining old French doctrines and practices (*subsidiarité*, mission command, and such modular task forces as the GTIA and SGTIA) rather than driving dramatically new concepts.

Despite these strategic dissimilarities, the French experience does show that there is almost certainly a value to NCW, at least against forces that do not possess sophisticated electronic warfare capabilities. Significant skepticism is merited, however, with respect to fighting those forces that do. One immediate and concrete takeaway for the U.S. Army is the imperative to "harden" its communications against electronic warfare as much as possible. In this report, we do not speculate about whether the cost of networking would be worth it solely for permissive environments, nor do we discuss the feasibility of sufficiently hardening communication systems, but these are areas where the French experience might be generalizable. Although the French Army has not actually fought an armor conflict in decades, the French experience also suggests that technological sophistication does not compensate for mass and protection, especially against more-capable adversaries.

Moreover, especially as the U.S. Army rethinks its military modernization approach with a new strategic direction (great power high-end conflict) and new structures (e.g., Army Futures Command), there are five important, if more abstract, lessons the U.S. Army can and should learn from the French example about how to approach military modernization more broadly.

Moderate Ambitions

One striking comparison between the French approach to NCW and the U.S. approach—particularly those of the late 1990s—is that the former has a more modest conception of what military modernization does and does not buy. As mentioned in Chapter Four, few French officers believed that NCW would transform warfare or how the French Army operates; rather, they simply believed that networked warfare technology would be an improvement over what they had, so they invested in it. The same could not be said of the U.S. network-centric theorists of the late 1990s. Nonetheless, the French Army's more modest, if incremental, approach to modernization seemingly has paid off (in the sense that the equipment is being fielded), whereas grander U.S. modernization plans have fallen flat.[3]

---

[3]   The best discussion of the failure of the U.S. Army's largest modernization program remains Pernin et al., 2012.

Weigh the Risks of Failure Versus Incompatibility

The French experience shows the value of moderating ambitions toward technology and it also highlights the trade-off inherent in incrementalism between the risks of failure and the risk of incompatibility. On one hand, the French Army's incremental approach to NEB likely saved it from making big, costly blunders up front. On the other hand, as the French Army learned, taking an incremental approach, particularly with communications technology, risks incompatibility and diminishes the overall effectiveness of the system. Consequently, the French Army adopted the more holistic and ambitious approach to modernization for NEB 2.0 with SCORPION—albeit after having experimented with the technology for roughly 15 years. Although it is too soon to tell whether betting big will ultimately pay off, at the very least, the French experience underscores that the U.S. Army leadership needs to weigh the pros and cons of incrementalism explicitly and up front in the procurement process.

Field and Test Early

One of the more impressive features of the French program is how quickly they began fielding equipment. Despite the fact that the French conception of NEB was developed only in the late 1990s, the French fielded the technology in Côte d'Ivoire by 2006. As discussed in Chapter Four, this allowed the French to inject real-world lessons learned into the design processes early on. The relatively speedy field-testing of the technology was made possible in part by the fact that Côte d'Ivoire was a comparatively permissive operating environment (relative to contemporaneous operations in Iraq and Afghanistan) and by the French tolerance for risk. Either way, the French modernization program benefited from these experiences, and to the extent that operational conditions allow, the U.S. Army should follow a similar approach.

Anticipate the Human Dimension of Technology

One of the greatest challenges in the French adoption of NEB has been integrating technology with the human dimension. Some of the lessons here are self-evident: Technology that is easy to use gets used, and soldiers like modularity because it allows for greater operational flexibility. Perhaps the most interesting example to a U.S. observer is how the French have struggled to marry NEB with preexisting cultural norms of *rusticité*—one's ability to rough it—and *subsidiarité*, or decentralized command and control. Although French officers have differing opinions about NEB's precise effect on these cultural norms, for the most part they acknowledge that the two have a symbiotic relationship: Technology can change institutional culture, and institutional culture can shape how technology is used.

Although the U.S. Army has different institutional norms than its French counterpart, the need to think about the human and cultural implications of technology remains the same. After all, communications technology does not simply affect how units exchange information with each other and up and down the chain of command; it also affects how leaders exercise command and control, how units operate, and, ultimately, how soldiers fight. The French experience reinforces the importance of considering these second-order effects as part of the development process.

Know How to Fight Without the Technology

Finally, as much as this report has focused on the French Army's adoption of NCW—NEB and SCORPION—the French experience also underscores the importance of not becoming overly reliant on this technology. As discussed earlier, the French Army historically has prided itself on *rusticité*, or being able to make do in difficult circumstances, often in poor conditions and with inadequate resources. Whether the French Army will be able to retain this virtue as successive generations of soldiers become increasingly comfortable with and dependent on the technology remains an open question. As French Army officers noted, though, instilling *rusticité* in future generations is more than just a question of preserving a cultural norm; it is an operational imperative. If indeed the future of warfare includes high-end conflict, forces need to be able fight in a degraded environment. Similarly, although the U.S. Army lacks an explicit norm of *rusticité,* the same operational imperative—to be able to fight without technology if need be—applies, especially as part of the Army's renewed emphasis on preparing for conflict with near-peer adversaries.

Ultimately, the French experience with NCW may do little to relieve the U.S. military's—and particularly, the U.S. Army's—skepticism about the concept or to reincarnate some of the grand promises of the 1990s-era RMA. However, it confirms that at least some aspects of the technology's presumed advantages are valid or might yet prove valid: The technology does enhance French Army capabilities, and the French appear to believe that it might do so even more as the technology matures. But it will take time, far more time than the U.S. theorists of the 1990s or the FCS program advocates imagined. In this light, the incrementalism of the French approach reveals itself to be particularly valid, and the French experience with NEB and SCORPION provides an instructive case study for the U.S. Army.

References

Adams, Thomas K., *The Army After Next: The First Postindustrial Army*, Stanford, Calif.: Stanford University Press, 2008.

Alberts, David S., John J. Garstka, and Frederick P. Stein, *Network Centric Warfare: Developing and Leveraging Information Superiority*, 2nd ed., Washington, D.C.: C4ISR Cooperative Research Program, 2000.

Asencio, Michel, *Les opérations en réseau: Vision d'ensemble*, Fondation pour la Recherche Stratégique, No. 3, 2009.

Barnett, Thomas P. M., "The Seven Deadly Sins of Network-Centric Warfare," *Proceedings*, Vol. 125, No. 1, January 1999.

Bezacier, Gérard, "La Transformation," *Doctrine: Revue militaire générale de l'armée de terre française*, No. 1, December 2003, pp. 4–7.

Brown, John Sloan, *Kevlar Legions: The Transformation of the U.S. Army, 1989–2005*, Washington, D.C.: United States Army Center for Military History, 2011.

Brustlein, Corentin, *Maîtriser la puissance de feu: Un défi pour les forces terrestres*, Paris: Institut Français des Relations Internationales, 2015.

Bush, George W., "A Period of Consequences," speech delivered at the Citadel, Military College of South Carolina, September 23, 1999. As of April 15, 2019:
http://www.citadel.edu/root/pres_bush

———, "U.S. President George W. Bush Addresses the Corps of Cadets," speech delivered at the Citadel, Military College of South Carolina, December 12, 2001. As of April 15, 2019:
http://www.citadel.edu/root/presbush01

Cabirol, Michel, "Défense: Cassidian n'a pas vu arriver Bull-dozer," *La Tribune*, April 19, 2013. As of April 29, 2019:
https://www.latribune.fr/entreprises-finance/industrie/aeronautique-defense/20130417trib000760033/defense-cassidian-n-a-pas-vu-arriver-bull-dozer-.html

———, "Défense: l'armée de Terre va enfin changer ses vieux 'chameaux,'" *La Tribune*, December 6, 2014. As of April 29, 2019:
https://www.latribune.fr/entreprises-finance/industrie/aeronautique-defense/20141206trib74266ca36/defense-l-armee-de-terre-va-enfin-changer-ses-vieux-chameaux.html

Caplain, Serge, "Les 10 pièges de la numérisation des forces terrestres," LinkedIn blog, January 15, 2018. As of April 2, 2019:
https://www.linkedin.com/pulse/les-10-pi%C3%A8ges-de-la-num%C3%A9risation-des-forces-serge-caplain/

Cebrowski, Arthur K., and John J. Garstka, "Network-Centric Warfare: Its Origin and Future," *Proceedings*, Vol. 124, January 1998.

Centre de Doctrine d'Emploi des Forces, "La transformation de 4 forces terrestres alliées: vers un modèle à la française?" *Héraclès*, Vol. 4, 2004.

———, *Des electrons et des hommes: Nouvelles technologies de l'information et conduite des opérations*, Cahier de la recherche doctrine, Paris, 2005.

———, *Des électrons dans la brousse: Premiers retours d'expérience de la numérisation de l'espace de bataille*, Cahiers du RETEX, Paris, 2007.

———, *Tactique Générale*, Paris: Armée de Terre, 2008.

———, *Principes d'organisation de commandement et d'emploi d'une force numérisée: Utilisation de la numérisation*, Paris: Ministère de la Defense, 2009.

———, *L'Armée de terre française 1978–2015: Bilan des 37 années d'opérations ininterrompue*, Cahiers du RETEX, Paris: Centre de Doctrine d'Emploi de Force, 2015.

Chaligne, Nicolas, "Le système d'information du combat SCORPION," *Fantassins*, No. 36, 2016, pp. 48–52. As of April 29, 2019:
http://www.emd.terre.defense.gouv.fr/img/emd/fantassin/2016_n36_fantassins.pdf

Chatelus, Franck, "Maîtriser la NEB pour accélérer la décision," *Doctrine Tactique*, No. 27, June 2013, pp. 24–28.

Collet-Billon, Laurent, *Audition de M. Laurent Collet-Billon, délégué général pour l'armement, sur le projet de loi de programmation militaire et le projet de loi de finances pour 2014*, Paris, France: Assemblée Nationale, October 2, 2013. As of June 26, 2018:
http://www.assemblee-nationale.fr/14/cr-cdef/13-14/c1314003.asp

Cotard, Eric, "NEB: de l'adolescence à la maturité," *Doctrine Tactique*, No. 27, June 2013, pp. 18–20.

Dahl, Erik J., "Network Centric Warfare and the Death of Operational Art," *Defence Studies*, Vol. 2, No. 1, 2002.

Desportes, Vincent, "Armées: 'Technologisme' ou 'Juste Technologie?'" *Politique étrangère*, No. 2, 2009, pp. 403–418.

———, *La Dernière Bataille de France: Lettre aux Français qui croient encore être défendus*, Paris: Gallimard, 2015.

Direction Générale de l'Armament, "Le ministère de la Défense commande les premiers véhicules blindés GRIFFON et JAGUAR du programme SCORPION," press release, April 22, 2017. As of April 29, 2019:
https://www.defense.gouv.fr/english/salle-de-presse/communiques/communiques-du-ministere-des-armees/cp-commande-des-premiers-vehicules-blindes-griffon-et-jaguar-programme-scorpion

DoD—*See* U.S. Department of Defense.

EADS Defense and Security Systems, "SIR (Regimental Information System)," *Defense Update*, No. 3, 2005. As of April 13, 2019:
https://defense-update.com/20060726_sir.html

Embassy of France in the United States, "France and Allies Reinforce Protection Measures in the Baltic Space," January 29, 2019. As of April 26, 2019:
https://franceintheus.org/spip.php?article8989

Espitalier, Marc, "Le chef et la machine," *Fantassins: Le magazine d'information de l'infanterie*, No. 36, 2016, pp. 21–28.

Feickert, Andrew, *The Army's Future Combat System (FCS): Background and Issues for Congress*, Washington, D.C.: Congressional Research Service, RL32888, April 28, 2005.

Forecast International, "FELIN," May 2009. As of April 20, 2019:
https://www.forecastinternational.com/archive/disp_pdf.cfm?DACH_RECNO=90

Gonzales, Dan, John S. Hollywood, Jerry M. Sollinger, James McFadden, John DeJarnette, Sara Harting, and Donald Temple, *Networked Forces in Stability Operations: 101st Airborne Division, 3/2 and 1/25 Stryker Brigades in Northern Iraq*, Santa Monica, Calif.: RAND Corporation, MG-593-OSD, 2007. As of April 29, 2019:
https://www.rand.org/pubs/monographs/MG593.html

Gonzales, Dan, Michael Johnson, Jimmie McEver, Dennis Leedom, Gina Kingston, and Michael S. Tang, *Network-Centric Operations Case Study: The Stryker Brigade Combat Team*, Santa Monica, Calif.: RAND Corporation, MG-267-1-OSD, 2005. As of April 28, 2019:
https://www.rand.org/pubs/monographs/MG267-1.html

Goya, Michel, "Dix ans d'expérience des brigades numérisées Stryker," *Lettre du Retex-Recherche*, No. 16, May 2014.

Gros, Philippe, Nicole Vilboux, Anne Kovacs, Frédéric Coste, Michel Klein, and Amélie Malissard, *Du Network-Centric à la Stabilisation: Émergence des "nouveaux" concepts et innovation militaire*, Études de l'IRSEM, Paris, France, No. 6, 2010.

Guibert, Nathalie, "'On ne peut pas faire la guerre contre le moral des soldats,'" *Le Monde*, July 1, 2010. As of April 29, 2019:
https://www.lemonde.fr/a-la-une/article/2010/07/01/general-vincent-desportes-on-ne-peut-pas-faire-la-guerre-contre-le-moral-des-soldats_1381645_3208.html?xtmc=desportes_afghanistan&xtcr=4

Guisnel, Jean, "Le programme Scorpion, ou l'avenir des armements terrestres français," *Le Point*, August 1, 2008. As of April 12, 2018:
http://www.lepoint.fr/actualites-monde/2008-08-01/le-programme-scorpion-ou-l-avenir-des-armements-terrestres/1648/0/264670

Hémez, Rémi, and Aline Leboeuf, *Retours sur Sangaris: Entre stabilisation et protection des civils*, Paris: Institut Français des Relations Internationales, 2016.

Hémez, Rémy, *L'Avenir de la surprise tactique à l'heure de la numérisation*, Paris: Institut Français des Relations Internationales, 2016.

Hertel, Olivier, "14 juillet: le Griffon, nouveau blindé high-tech de l'Armée de terre," *Sciences et Avenir*, July 14, 2017.

Huberdeau, Emmanuel, "Acceleration de la numérisation de l'ALAT," *Air & Cosmos*, December 7, 2017. As of March 30, 2018:
http://www.air-cosmos.com/acceleration-de-la-numerisation-de-l-alat-104245

Hubin, Guy, *Perspectives Tactiques*, 3rd ed., Paris: Economica, 2009.

Irondelle, Bastien, *La réforme des armées en France*, Paris: Presses de Sciences Po, 2011.

Jacops, Yves, "La NEB: limites et plus-values," *Doctrine Tactique*, No. 27, June 2013.

Johnson, Stuart, John E. Peters, Karin E. Kitchens, Aaron L. Martin, and Jordan R. Fischbach, *A Review of the Army's Modular Force Structure*, Santa Monica, Calif.: RAND Corporation, TR-927-2-OSD, 2012. As of August 5, 2019:
https://www.rand.org/pubs/technical_reports/TR927-2.html

Joint Chiefs of Staff, *Joint Vision 2020: America's Military—Preparing for Tomorrow*, Washington, D.C., 2000.

Klotz, Martin, "Les enjeux capacitaires de la numérisation de la NEB," *Doctrine Tactique*, No. 27, June 2013, pp. 6–8.

Krempff, Éléonore, "La révolution de l'armée de Terre en marche," *Armées d'aujourd'hui*, No. 390, June 2014.

Krepinevich, Andrew F., "Cavalry to Computer: The Pattern of Military Revolutions," *The National Interest*, October 1994.

Krepinevich, Andrew F., Jr., *The Military-Technical Revolution: A Preliminary Assessment*, Washington, D.C.: Center for Strategic and Budgetary Assessments, 2002.

Land Force, "Mag Terre Vidéo 47," YouTube, May 14, 2011. As of August 5, 2019:
https://www.youtube.com/watch?v=dWKiQNCdvGs

"L'Assemblée adopte le budget de la Défense pour 2018," *Le figaro économie*, November 8, 2017. As of July 9, 2018:
http://www.lefigaro.fr/conjoncture/2017/11/08/
20002-20171108ARTFIG00042-l-assemblee-adopte-le-budget-de-la-defense-pour-2018.php

Lauley, Roxane, *"Le programme Scorpion démarre,"* Enterprise Défense Relations Internationales, November 6, 2014. As of April 16, 2019:
https://www.enderi.fr/Le-programme-Scorpion-demarre_a237.html

Le Portail de l'Armement, "NEXTER SYSTEMS," homepage, undated. As of April 29, 2019:
https://www.nexter-group.fr/en/subsidiaries/nexter-systems

Lert, Frédéric, "SITALAT: les hélicoptères de l'ALAT connectés," *Air & Cosmos*, November 28, 2014. As of March 30, 2018:
http://www.air-cosmos.com/sitalat-les-helicopteres-de-l-alat-connectes-27120

Luddy, John, *The Challenge and Promise of Network-Centric Warfare*, Arlington, Va.: Lexington Institute, 2005.

Macgregor, Douglas A., *Breaking the Phalanx: A New Design for Landpower in the 21st Century*, Westport, Conn.: Greenwood Publishing Group, 1997.

Marshall, Andrew W., "Some Thoughts on Military Revolutions," ONA memorandum for record, July 27, 1993, p. 1.

———, "Some Thoughts on Military Revolutions—Second Version," ONA memorandum for record, August 23, 1993.

Meriau, Olivier, Anne-Henry Budan de Russé, and Rémi Pellabeuf, "Une approche pragmatique: la numérisation sur le théâtre afghan," *Doctrine Tactique*, No. 27, June 2013, pp. 42–46.

Ministère de la Défense, *Livre Blanc sur la Défense*, Paris: Ministère de la Défense, 1994.

Ministère des Armées, "Lancement du programme CONTACT de radio logicielle," webpage, April 20, 2012. As of March 30, 2018:
https://www.defense.gouv.fr/terre/actu-terre/archives/
lancement-du-programme-contact-de-radio-logicielle

———, "Programme Scorpion: lancement de la rénovation du char Leclerc," webpage, March 27, 2015. As of April 2, 2018:
https://www.defense.gouv.fr/espanol/dga/actualite/
programme-scorpion-lancement-de-la-renovation-du-char-leclerc

———, "SICF," webpage, July 4, 2016a. As of March 29, 2018:
https://www.defense.gouv.fr/terre/equipements/materiels-generiques/
commandement-transmissions/sicf

———, "Le système ATLAS," webpage, July 13, 2016b. As of April 10, 2018:
https://www.defense.gouv.fr/terre/equipements/materiels-specifiques/
artillerie/acquisition/le-systeme-atlas

———, "La 3D se numérise," webpage, September 5, 2016c. As of March 30, 2018:
https://www.defense.gouv.fr/terre/actu-terre/la-3d-se-numerise

———, "Scorpion: Commande des premiers véhicules blindés VBMR et EBRC," webpage, July 5,
2017. As of March 28, 2018:
https://www.defense.gouv.fr/dga/actualite/
scorpion-commande-des-premiers-vehicules-blindes-vbmr-et-ebrc

———, "CP_Developpement du véhicule blindé multi-rôles léger," webpage, February 12, 2018. As
of March 30, 2018:
https://www.defense.gouv.fr/actualites/operations/
cp_developpement-du-vehicule-blinde-multi-roles-leger

Murdock, Paul, "Principles of War on the Network-Centric Battlefield: Mass and Economy of
Force," *Parameters*, Vol. 32, No. 1, Spring 2002.

Nardulli, Bruce R., Walter L. Perry, Bruce R. Pirnie, John Gordon IV, and John G. McGinn,
Disjointed War: Military Operations in Kosovo, 1999, Santa Monica, Calif.: RAND Corporation,
MR-1406-A, 2002. As of August 6, 2019:
https://www.rand.org/pubs/monograph_reports/MR1406.html

Nexter Group, "SCORPION Programme: LECLERC Tank Renovation Launched," press release,
March 12, 2015. As of March 30, 2018:
http://www.nexter-group.fr/en/press/
700-programme-scorpion-lancement-de-la-renovation-du-char-leclerc

O'Rourke, Ronald, *Navy Network-Centric Warfare Concept: Key Programs and Issues for Congress*,
Washington, D.C.: Congressional Research Service, RS20557, May 31, 2005.

Pearson, Taylor, "The Ultimate Guide to the OODA Loop," webpage, undated. As of April 24, 2019:
https://taylorpearson.me/ooda-loop/

Pernin, Christopher G., Elliot Axelband, Jeffrey A. Drezner, Brian Barber Dille, John Gordon IV,
Bruce J. Held, K. Scott McMahon, Walter L. Perry, Christopher Rizzi, Akhil R. Shah, Peter A.
Wilson, and Jerry M. Sollinger, *Lessons from the Army's Future Combat Systems Program*, Santa
Monica, Calif.: RAND Corporation, MG-1206-A, 2012. As of April 19, 2019:
https://www.rand.org/pubs/monographs/MG1206.html

Petit, Pierre, "Griffon et Jaguar au cœur de SCORPION," Defense24.news, February 20, 2018. As of
April 29, 2019:
http://www.defense24.news/2018/02/20/12015/amp/?__twitter_impression=true

Préfet de la Drôme, "GAMSTAT–Chabeuil," webpage, February 8, 2013. As of April 10, 2018:
http://www.drome.gouv.fr/gamstat-chabeuil-a3502.html

Rumsfeld, Donald H., "Transforming the Military," *Foreign Affairs*, Vol. 81, No. 3, May/June 2002.

Safran, "Soldier Modernization," webpage, undated. As of March 30, 2018:
https://www.safran-group.com/defense/soldier-modernization

———, "Sagem Receives 500 New Orders for SITEL Tactical Information Systems for French
Army," press release, October 6, 2009. As of March 30, 2018:
https://www.safran-group.com/media/
20091006_sagem-receives-500-new-orders-sitel-tactical-information-systems-french-army

—————, "Boar's Head Exercise with the British Army: FELIN Makes European Début," press release, April 12, 2012. As of March 30, 2018:
https://www.safran-electronics-defense.com/
media/20120412_boarhead-exercice-british-army-felin-makes-european-debut

—————, "Sagem Signs Major Contract To Upgrade French Army's FELIN Soldier Modernization System," press release, April 3, 2015. As of March 30, 2018:
https://www.safran-group.com/media/
20150403_sagem-signs-major-contract-upgrade-french-armys-felin-soldier-modernization-system

Sénat, Projet de loi de finances pour 2012: Défense: équipement des forces, 2011. As of March 29, 2018:
http://www.senat.fr/rap/a11-108-6/a11-108-610.html

—————, Projet de loi de finances pour 2013: Défense: équipement des forces, 2012. As of March 29, 2018:
http://www.senat.fr/rap/a12-150-8/a12-150-813.html

Shinseki, Eric K., address during the Eisenhower Luncheon of the 45th Annual Meeting of the Association of the United States Army, Washington, D.C., October 12, 1999.

"'Shock and Awe' Campaign Underway in Iraq," CNN Student News, March 22, 2003. As of April 15, 2019:
http://edition.cnn.com/2003/fyi/news/03/22/iraq.war/

Shurkin, Michael, France's War in Mali: Lessons for an Expeditionary Army, Santa Monica, Calif.: RAND Corporation, RR-770-A, 2014. As of April 22, 2019:
https://www.rand.org/pubs/research_reports/RR770.html

—————, "What a 1963 Novel Tells Us About the French Army, Mission Command, and the Romance of the Indochina War," War on the Rocks, September 20, 2017. As of April 29, 2019:
https://warontherocks.com/2017/09/what-a-1963-novel-tells-us-about-the-french-army-mission-command-and-the-romance-of-the-indochina-war/

—————, "Meet France's War Philosophers," War on the Rocks, January 5, 2018. As of April 29, 2019:
https://warontherocks.com/2018/01/meet-frances-war-philosophers/

Smith, Edward A., Jr., "Network-Centric Warfare: What's the Point?" Naval War College Review, Vol. 54, No. 1, Winter 2001, pp. 59–75.

Stein, Fred, John Garska, and Philip L. McIndoo, "Network-Centric Warfare: Impact on Army Operations," IEEE/AFCEA EUROCOMM 2000: Information Systems for Enhanced Public Safety and Security Proceedings, 2000, pp. 288–295.

Tenenbaum, Elie, The Battle Over Fire Support: The CAS Challenge and the Future of Artillery, Paris: Institut Français des Relations Internationales, 2012.

Thales, "Thalès proposera le premier système d'information et de commandement interopérable pour l'Armée de Terre et la Marine Française," press release, February 16, 2016. As of March 29, 2018:
https://www.thalesgroup.com/fr/worldwide/defense/press-release/
thales-proposera-le-premier-systeme-dinformation-et-de-commandement

—————, "Savez-vous qui sont le VBMR et l'EBRC?" webpage, January 12, 2015. As of April 2, 2018:
https://www.thalesgroup.com/fr/worldwide/defense/case-study/savez-vous-qui-sont-griffon-et-jaguar

TRADOC—See U.S. Army Training and Doctrine Command.

Tran, Pierre, "Meet Serval, France's Next Multi-Role Armoured Vehicle," *DefenseNews*, June 11, 2018. As of April 29, 2019:
https://www.defensenews.com/digital-show-dailies/eurosatory/2018/06/12/meet-serval-frances-next-multi-role-armoured-vehicle/

United Nations Interim Force in Lebanon, "UNIFIL Troop-Contributing Countries," webpage, November 30, 2018. As of December 14, 2018:
https://unifil.unmissions.org/unifil-troop-contributing-countries

U.S. Army Training and Doctrine Command, *Force XXI Operations: A Concept for the Evolution of Full-Dimensional Operations for the Strategic Army of the Early Twenty-First Century*, Fort Monroe, Va., TRADOC Pamphlet 525-5, 1994.

U.S. Army Training and Doctrine Command Military History Office, *TRADOC Annual Command History 1999-2000*, Fort Eustis, Va.: United States Army Training and Doctrine Command, 2006.

U.S. Department of the Army, *Counterinsurgency*, Washington, D.C., Field Manual 3-24, December 2006.

U.S. Department of Defense, *Summary of the 2018 National Defense Strategy of the United States of America: Sharpening the American Military's Competitive Edge*, Washington, D.C., January 2018. As of April 18, 2019:
https://dod.defense.gov/Portals/1/Documents/pubs/2018-National-Defense-Strategy-Summary.pdf

Vaizand, Jean-François, "La minsitre des Armées chez Nexter pour une nouvelle commande," *L'Essor*, February 15, 2018.

White, Andrew, "Thales Readies Antares for French Army," *Jane's International Defence Review*, February 14, 2018.

Wilson, Clay, *Network Centric Operations: Background and Oversight Issues for Congress*, Washington, D.C.: Congressional Research Service, RL32411, March 15, 2007.

Yakovleff, Michel, *Tactique Théorique*, 3rd ed., Paris: Economica, 2016.